Parkinson's Disease

Lizabeth Craig

LUCENT BOOKS

A part of Gale, Cengage Learning

GALE
CENGAGE Learning·

Farmington Hills, Mich • San Francisco • New York • Waterville, Maine
Meriden, Conn • Mason, Ohio • Chicago

LIBRARY OF CONGRESS CATALOGING-IN-PUBLICATION DATA

Craig, Lizabeth.
  Parkinson's disease / by Lizabeth Craig.
    pages cm. -- (Diseases & disorders)
  Summary: "This title in Lucent's Diseases and Disorders series focuses on Parkinson's Disease. The book describes how the disease is contracted, its symptoms, and treatments. It also discusses the issues that caregivers face"-- Provided by publisher.
  Includes bibliographical references and index.
  ISBN 978-1-4205-1227-4 (hardback)
  1. Parkinson's disease. I. Title.
  RC382.C913 2015
  616.8'33--dc23
                                                            2014033542

Lucent Books
27500 Drake Rd.
Farmington Hills, MI 48331

ISBN-13: 978-1-4205-1227-4
ISBN-10: 1-4205-1227-7

Printed in the United States of America
1 2 3 4 5 6 7 19 18 17 16 15

Table of Contents

"The Most Difficult Puzzles Ever Devised"

Charles Best, one of the pioneers in the search for a cure for diabetes, once explained what it is about medical research that intrigued him so. "It's not just the gratification of knowing one is helping people," he confided, "although that probably is a more heroic and selfless motivation. Those feelings may enter in, but truly, what I find best is the feeling of going toe to toe with nature, of trying to solve the most difficult puzzles ever devised. The answers are there somewhere, those keys that will solve the puzzle and make the patient well. But how will those keys be found?"

Since the dawn of civilization, nothing has so puzzled people—and often frightened them, as well—as the onset of illness in a body or mind that had seemed healthy before. A seizure, the inability of a heart to pump, the sudden deterioration of muscle tone in a small child—being unable to reverse such conditions or even to understand why they occur was unspeakably frustrating to healers. Even before there were names for such conditions, even before they were understood at all, each was a reminder of how complex the human body was, and how vulnerable.

While our grappling with understanding diseases has been frustrating at times, it has also provided some of humankind's most heroic accomplishments. Alexander Fleming's accidental discovery in 1928 of a mold that could be turned into penicillin has resulted in the saving of untold millions of lives. The isolation of the enzyme insulin has reversed what was once a death sentence for anyone with diabetes. There have been great strides in combating conditions for which there is not yet a cure, too. Medicines can help AIDS patients live longer, diagnostic tools such as mammography and ultrasounds can help doctors find tumors while they are treatable, and laser surgery techniques have made the most intricate, minute operations routine.

This "toe-to-toe" competition with diseases and disorders is even more remarkable when seen in a historical continuum. An astonishing amount of progress has been made in a very short time. Just two hundred years ago, the existence of germs as a cause of some diseases was unknown. In fact, it was less than 150 years ago that a British surgeon named Joseph Lister had difficulty persuading his fellow doctors that washing their hands before delivering a baby might increase the chances of a healthy delivery (especially if they had just attended to a diseased patient)!

Each book in Lucent's Diseases and Disorders series explores a disease or disorder and the knowledge that has been accumulated (or discarded) by doctors through the years. Each book also examines the tools used for pinpointing a diagnosis, as well as the various means that are used to treat or cure a disease. Finally, new ideas are presented—techniques or medicines that may be on the horizon.

Frustration and disappointment are still part of medicine, for not every disease or condition can be cured or prevented. But the limitations of knowledge are being pushed outward constantly; the "most difficult puzzles ever devised" are finding challengers every day.

The Shaking Palsy

The year 1794 was a chaotic time of political reform and change in England. The people were very unhappy with the way their government was treating them. On top of that, the king himself was battling bouts of mental illness. Adding to his many headaches was the appearance of a series of pamphlets calling for political and social reforms, written by an unknown person who called himself simply "Old Hubert." Later that year several members of a secret political group in London were brought before the government to answer charges of plotting to assassinate the king. Nicknamed the "Pop Gun Plot," its goal had been to use a poisoned dart from an air gun to end the king's reign early. One of the men called to testify was a surgeon and scientist named James Parkinson. Under intense questioning, he finally admitted to being the mysterious Old Hubert.

Fortunately for Parkinson, the Pop Gun Plot was soon forgotten, and no charges were filed against him. Even so, he gave up his political activities and turned his attention back to health and medicine. In the early 1800s one of his many interests centered on his observations of people with a disorder commonly called the "shaking palsy." Parkinson observed six sufferers of this malady (several of whom he simply met at random on the street) and wrote about their symptoms. In his 1817 work, "An Essay on the Shaking Palsy," Parkinson described tremors of the hands and legs, a stooped-over posture, muscle rigidity, and a shuffling kind of gait while walking. At the time, the essay received little attention. By the end of the century, however, the shaking palsy would have a new name.

An Ancient Malady

The signs and symptoms of the shaking palsy, which today is called Parkinson's disease (or PD for short), had been known for a very long time. As far back as 5000 B.C., a medical text from ancient East Indian Ayurvedic medicine described symptoms of a shaking illness called "Kampavata." Kampavata was treated with a tropical bean-like plant called *Mucuna pruriens*, or velvet bean, which contains a chemical very similar to levodopa—the most common modern drug used to treat PD. Preparations of velvet bean are still used in some parts of the world to treat symptoms of PD.

The earliest known Chinese medical document, the twenty-five-hundred-year-old *Huang Di Nei Jing Su Wen*, includes a description of a PD-like illness. In the eighth-century-B.C. Greek epic poem the *Iliad*, elderly King Nestor laments that he can no longer participate in competitions: "My limbs are no longer steady, dear friend; nor my feet, neither do my arms, as they once did, swing light from my shoulders."[1] The Greek physician Erasistratus of Ceos (310–250 B.C.) wrote of a kind of paralysis that he called *paradoxos*, in which a person stops walking and cannot seem to start again, a common sign of PD. One of the most famous of ancient Greek physicians, Galen (A.D. 129–200), wrote extensively about motor disorders, including tremors of the hands when at rest, muscle rigidity, and inability to control movements in the elderly—all signs of PD. He is credited with coining the term *shaking palsy* to refer to these symptoms. The term was used to refer to the disease for the next seventeen hundred years.

Descriptions of PD-like disorders appear in many writings all throughout the Middle Ages and the Renaissance (from about 450 to 1550). One of history's most famous medieval physicians was Ibn Sina of Persia, also known as Avicenna (980–1037). His great medical work, *The Canon of Medicine*, includes extensive coverage of movement and nervous disorders, including

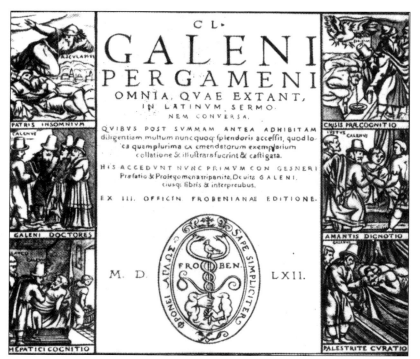

Second-century A.D. Greek physician Galen wrote about motor disorders, hand tremors, and the inability to control muscle movements as the "shaking palsy." He may have been describing Parkinson's disease.

various treatments. In the late fifteenth century, the Italian artist and scientist Leonardo da Vinci (1452–1519) wrote in a letter about uncontrollable movements that "appear clearly in paralytics . . . who move their trembling limbs such as the head or the hands without permission of the soul; which soul with all its power cannot prevent these limbs from trembling."[2] Many other authors, physicians, and scientists throughout the sixteenth, seventeenth, and eighteenth centuries mentioned disorders that sound very much like PD. For example, in his 1591 play *Henry VI*, English playwright William Shakespeare (1564–1616) included a character who explains that his shaking is caused not by fear but by "palsy." Scottish surgeon John Hunter (1728–1793) may have been referring to PD when he noticed that even patients with severe tremors never complained about the muscles involved feeling tired. "For instance," he wrote, "Lord L's hands are almost perpetually in motion, and he never feels the sensation of them being tired. When he is asleep, his hands, etc. are perfectly at rest, but when he wakes, in a little while they begin to move."[3] In attendance at one of Hunter's lectures in 1785 was a young student named James Parkinson.

Lectures by Scots surgeon John Hunter (shown) inspired his student James Parkinson to do further research on the disease that would be named for Parkinson.

Still a Mystery

A tremendous amount has been learned about PD since James Parkinson's day, but in many respects, PD is still somewhat of a mystery to many physicians and their patients. It includes dozens of different signs and symptoms, many of which appear in some patients but not in others. The same symptom may be worse in one patient than in another, and over time the disease may worsen more rapidly in some than in others. Several other disorders have similar symptoms, so it can be misdiagnosed as something else. The illness can often go completely undiagnosed because many people believe that their symptoms are just a normal part of growing older. Some scientists and physicians question whether it can really be called a true disease—a condition with clear causes, symptoms, and treatments.

PD strikes people of all backgrounds and socioeconomic levels. Many well-known people have been afflicted with PD, including Pope John Paul II, former U.S. attorney general Janet Reno, Canadian prime minister Pierre Trudeau, evangelist Billy Graham, singer Linda Ronstadt, actor Michael J. Fox, and German dictator Adolf Hitler. PD usually affects older people, but it can occur earlier in life. It is very rare in people under age thirty. The average age of onset is about sixty, and it affects about one person in every twenty over age eighty. It is slightly more common in men than in women, and although it occurs in all races, it is somewhat more common in Caucasians (whites). According to the Parkinson's Disease Foundation, PD affects about 1 million people in the United States and an estimated 7 to 10 million people worldwide. Approximately sixty thousand Americans are diagnosed with PD each year, but it is suspected that thousands more go undetected. As the average age of the American population continues to increase, the incidence of PD is expected to rise accordingly. While PD itself is not a fatal illness, problems caused by the disease make PD the fourteenth leading cause of death in the United States, according to the Centers for Disease Control and Prevention.

Because of its chronic (long-term) nature, PD can be a very costly illness. According to the Parkinson's Disease Foundation, the total cost to the U.S. economy in expenses related to PD—including treatment, Social Security payments, and lost income due to inability to work—approaches $14 billion per year. Medication costs for a person with PD average about $2,500 a year, and surgical treatments can cost up to $100,000.

A Life-Changing Diagnosis

A diagnosis of PD usually means that significant changes in a person's daily life will need to be made. Almost every aspect of daily living is affected. Many of the things a person always took for granted—such as eating, bathing, driving, walking, and even writing—become a challenge. Safety in the home is a major issue. Emotional and psychological changes accompany the physical ones, presenting additional challenges for patients and their caregivers (who must also make many changes and adaptations in their own lives). There is as yet no cure for PD, but the good news is that Parkinson's disease usually progresses slowly. It can be many years, even decades, from first diagnosis until the person experiences significant disability. There are many ways to treat and manage the symptoms that can help make life easier for patients and their families. Dozens of support groups and organizations exist to help patients and their families learn about PD and how to live with it so that simple pleasures can remain a part of everyday life.

CHAPTER ONE

What Is Parkinson's Disease?

In October 1994 life was looking pretty good for Lieutenant Colonel Michael R. "Rich" Clifford. A 1974 graduate of the U.S. Military Academy at West Point, he had gone on to graduate at the top of his class at the U.S. Army Aviation School. In 1986 he became an army test pilot, and the following year he was assigned to the Johnson Space Center, working with NASA's space shuttle program. In 1990 he was selected to be an astronaut. Two years later he flew his first space shuttle mission.

Six months after his second mission, in 1994, he went in for a routine physical exam. Everything checked out fine, but he did have one minor issue. He says:

> Just as a favor, I asked the flight surgeon . . . if I could have an orthopedic surgeon look at my right shoulder. He asked me where it hurt and I told him it didn't hurt at all. Rather, my right arm just seemed to hang without moving when I walked. I could tell I must have touched a nerve because he immediately called for the Chief Flight Surgeon. The chief asked me to walk with him down the hall. Little did I know how that walk would change my life.[4]

A whirlwind of specialists and tests followed, after which Clifford was informed that he had Parkinson's disease. The diagnosis came as a complete surprise to Clifford. "I had never

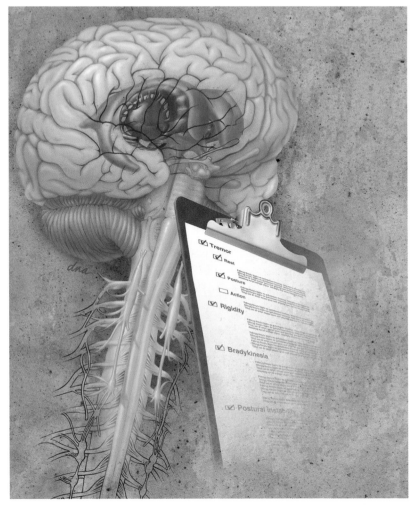

Parkinson's disease is a chronic, progressive, degenerative disease
of the brain. The illustration highlights the areas of the brain
affected by this neurologic disorder.

heard of this disease and as someone who considered himself
to be in excellent physical condition, I naturally assumed it
was something I could conquer. . . . My only symptom was
that my right arm didn't move when I walked. It seemed impossible. I didn't want to believe it, and for a while I refused
to believe it."[5]

It is not surprising that Clifford had a hard time accepting a diagnosis of Parkinson's disease. Most people, if they have even heard of PD, think of it as a disease of older people. Clifford was only forty-two at the time of his diagnosis. Although PD has been known for a very long time, and although it is fairly common, most patients and their families, upon hearing the diagnosis, ask, "What *is* Parkinson's disease?"

Parkinson's disease is a chronic, progressive, degenerative neurologic disease of the brain. Chronic diseases last a long time; PD lasts for the rest of the person's life. A progressive disease is one in which the symptoms get worse over time. PD tends to go through several stages of increasingly disabling symptoms as it progresses. Degenerative diseases are those that lead to a steady decrease in the person's ability to function, and neurologic diseases affect the nervous system. Therefore, PD is a lifelong illness that gets worse over time, affects the brain, and may eventually interfere significantly with a person's ability to carry out activities of daily living.

PD is called a disorder of movement because its four major symptoms involve problems with movements. These are tremors (uncontrollable trembling of small muscles), muscle rigidity or stiffness, bradykinesia (slowness of movement), and postural instability (problems with walking, balancing, and standing). PD is the most common of a group of movement disorders with a similar set of symptoms, which collectively are called parkinsonism or parkinsonian syndrome. People with Parkinson's disease have parkinsonism, but not all people with parkinsonism have Parkinson's disease; several other disorders besides PD cause parkinsonism. Parkinsonism may be caused by strokes, head injuries, certain medications, illegal drug use, or other degenerative neurological diseases that produce the same kinds of movement problems. This is one reason why PD can be so difficult to diagnose correctly.

How a Body Moves

Every movement of the human body, from turning a cartwheel or a somersault to blinking the eyes, is controlled by the brain. The brain is by far the most complex human organ. It controls

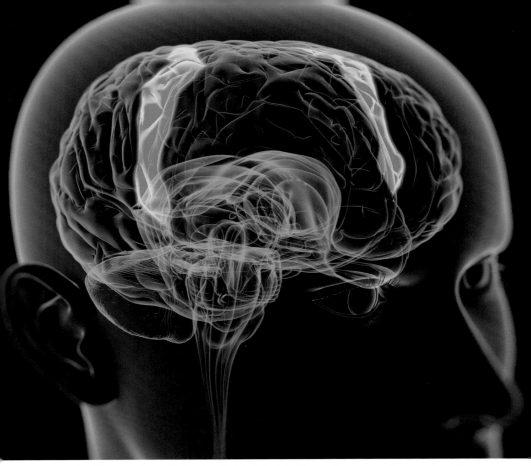

An illustration of the brain highlights the primary motor cortex. It works with the pre-motor areas to plan and execute movements.

every function that the body does, including digestion, heartbeat, breathing, and interpreting input from the five senses. It is responsible for every thought people have, everything they learn and remember, and every decision they make. Scientists used to consider the brain unknowable, but thanks to rapid advances in brain research in the 1990s, scientists have learned more about the inner workings of the brain in the last twenty years than in all the centuries before. In fact, the U.S. Congress named the 1990s the Decade of the Brain.

Several parts of the brain have important roles in controlling body movements. The cerebral cortex—the large, grayish-white, "wrinkly" part of the brain—has many functions, including controlling voluntary movements of the body. Voluntary movements are those that a person makes a conscious decision to do. They are controlled by a section of the cerebral cortex called the motor cortex. Every time a person raises an arm, takes a step, kicks a ball, dances, runs, or kisses a puppy, the motor cortex makes it happen.

James Parkinson

James Parkinson was born in 1755 in Shoreditch, London, England. His father was an apothecary (a preparer of medicines, similar to a pharmacist) and a surgeon. In 1784 James also became a surgeon and took over his father's surgical practice after his father died. (At that time surgeons were considered to be different from physicians; Parkinson never became a physician and so is not referred to as "Dr. Parkinson.") He married and eventually had six children. Parkinson was interested in a wide variety of subjects besides medicine, such as geology, paleontology, and politics. He spoke out for the poor and underprivileged and was an outspoken critic of the British government of the time. He was involved in several secret antigovernment societies, calling for social reforms and more political rights for the poor, and wrote critical pamphlets under the name "Old Hubert." After being questioned about his involvement in an attempt to assassinate King George III, he left politics and returned to medicine. He remained concerned with the welfare of the poor, however, studying and writing on common maladies such as gout, appendicitis, and peritonitis (inflammation of the lining of the abdomen). He advocated for legal protection for the mentally ill and worked at a mental asylum for thirty years. He also worked to improve the welfare of working children.

Despite his many, varied activities, interests, and publications, he is best known for his "Essay on the Shaking Palsy," which he called "paralysis agitans." Not until after his death in 1824, however, was the illness renamed Parkinson's disease by the French neurologist Jean-Martin Charcot.

The cerebellum, located below and behind the cerebrum, is responsible for balance, timing, and coordination of movement. It makes it possible for a person to balance on one foot, hit a baseball, walk in a straight line, ride a bicycle, or turn around in a circle. The cerebellum also stores memories of movements, which is why people do not have to relearn how to ride a bike or play the piano once they have already learned it.

The brain stem, located at the very back of the brain just above the spinal cord, directs all the involuntary movements of the body. Involuntary movements are movements that a person is not always aware of and does not have to make a conscious decision to do, such as breathing, contractions of the heart muscle, and movement of food through the digestive system.

The area of the brain affected in Parkinson's disease is called the substantia nigra. The name is Latin for "black substance," because the cells in this area are dark in color. There are two parts of the substantia nigra, one on each side of the brain, but they are usually referred to as if they were one structure. The substantia nigra is a very small area, located deep within the base of the brain and close to the center. It is one of a collection of small structures called the basal ganglia. The basal ganglia act as a sort of motor filter, preventing the body from doing movements when they are not appropriate. They also communicate messages about movement to other parts of the brain.

Communication in the Brain

The brain is made up of several different kinds of cells, but the main kind of brain cell is called a neuron. All the activities of the brain result from electrical "messages" passed back and forth between neurons and between neurons and other kinds of cells. Specialized neurons with specific functions are located all throughout the body. For example, neurons that communicate with muscle cells and are involved in muscle movement are called motor neurons.

Neurons have three main parts. The cell body contains the nucleus of the cell, which is like the "command center" of the cell and directs all its functions. The cell body is surrounded by tiny projections called dendrites, which receive messages from other neurons. Electrical messages travel from the dendrites, through the nucleus, and leave the neuron through a tail-like projection called an axon. The message is then sent on to another cell—maybe another neuron, or a muscle cell, or a cell in another organ—and tells the next cell what to do.

The space between the axon and the next cell is called the synapse (SIN-aps). The synapse is the actual place where messages are passed between the neuron and the receiving cells, using a complex set of electrical and chemical events. When an electrical message (called an action potential) reaches the end of an axon, it stimulates the release of a special chemical called a neurotransmitter. The neurotransmitter crosses the synapse, binds to the next cell, and allows it to receive the message. After the action potential has been passed, the neurotransmitter is reabsorbed by the first cell so it is available for the next action potential. There are several kinds of neurotransmitters, each with its own functions. The symptoms of PD result from a lack of a neurotransmitter called dopamine (DOH-pa-meen). Among other things, dopamine is necessary for controlled movements of the muscles.

Dopamine

Dopamine is one of a number of neurotransmitters—chemicals that are responsible for carrying messages between neurons and other cells. Neurotransmitters, including dopamine, are made in specialized neurons in the brain that release their particular neurotransmitter whenever they are activated. Neurons that produce dopamine are called dopaminergic neurons. There are normally about four hundred thousand dopaminergic neurons, located in several parts of the brain. Most of them are located in the substantia nigra. Dopamine is found in the brain of almost all animals, from primitive reptiles up to human beings. It can also be found circulating through the body in the blood, but its function outside the brain is not clear. The function of dopamine in the brain was discovered in 1958 by Swedish scientists Arvid Carlsson and Nils-Åke Hillarp.

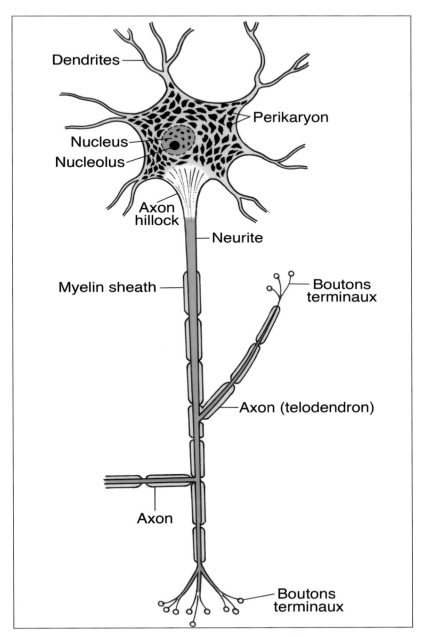

An illustration of a neuron. All the activities of the brain result from electrical "messages" passed back and forth between neurons and between neurons and other kinds of cells.

Dopamine has several interesting and seemingly unrelated functions in the human brain. One of these is called reward-motivated behavior. This means that dopamine is part of a brain "circuit" that motivates a person to seek pleasure and then uses the pleasure experienced as a reward that reinforces the behavior. For example, if a person has a "craving" for something sweet or salty, it is because dopamine has been released and is causing the person to seek something sugary or salty to eat, like a cupcake or a bag of chips. When the person

Neurotransmitters

Dopamine is just one of a number of very important brain chemicals called neurotransmitters. These specialized chemicals are responsible for carrying electrical nerve impulses between neurons in the brain and between neurons and other cells of the body. The function of neurotransmitters was discovered in 1936 by English pharmacologist Henry Dale and German pharmacologist Otto Loewi. The first one to be discovered was acetylcholine, mainly responsible for stimulating smooth muscle such as that in the stomach, intestinal tract, and bladder. Since then, about fifty different neurotransmitters have been identified. Imbalances in neurotransmitters can significantly impact the entire nervous system.

Neurotransmitters generally fall into one of three categories—amino acids, peptides, and monoamines. Examples of amino acids include glutamate and gamma-aminobutyric acid (GABA). Peptides are most active in the intestinal, urinary, reproductive, and circulatory systems and include vasopressin, oxytocin, and glucagon. Important monoamines include serotonin, melatonin, epinephrine (adrenaline), and histamine.

Some neurotransmitters are excitatory, which means they excite or stimulate the brain. Examples include epinephrine, known as the "fight-or-flight" chemical, and glutamate, which has a role in learning and memory and is the most abundant excitatory

gets it, the pleasure of eating it stimulates the release of more dopamine. Dopamine is released when a music lover goes to a concert, when an art lover looks at a beautiful painting, or when a fitness buff has a good workout. It is released in the brains of thrill seekers when they participate in a risky activity like skydiving. It is what drives athletes to compete and win. It is what motivates workers to do a good job so they will feel successful. When something is pleasurable, dopamine makes the person want to repeat the experience. In short, dopamine

neurotransmitter. Others are called inhibitory because they calm the brain. Examples include GABA, which calms anxiety, and serotonin and melatonin, which help regulate moods and the sleep-wake cycle. Dopamine is unusual in that it can be both excitatory and inhibitory.

Neurotransmitters carry electrical nerve impulses between neurons across the synapses, or spaces, between them.

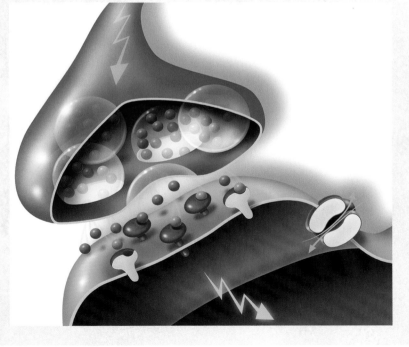

helps regulate behavior by motivating a person to seek pleasurable experiences and then reinforcing the desire to repeat the experience. The down side of this, however, is that it also motivates and rewards dangerous or unhealthy behaviors that may produce pleasure for some people, such as smoking, drug use, binge eating, or gambling.

Another role of dopamine is in cognitive, or mental, functions such as memory, problem solving, decision making, focus, and attention. A decrease in dopamine in the front part of the brain is thought to contribute to attention deficit disorder. Imbalances in dopamine are involved in certain psychological disorders such as social anxiety or depression (not enough dopamine) and in aggression, schizophrenia, or bipolar mania (too much dopamine). Dopamine is also necessary for the production of adrenaline (the "fight-or-flight" hormone) in the adrenal glands, and it slows the release of the hormone prolactin, which causes milk production in female mammals.

The function of dopamine that is of most importance to PD patients is in motor control—the coordination of body movements. Adequate levels of dopamine are necessary in order for messages from the brain to be communicated properly to the muscles. When these messages are not communicated properly, the movement problems of PD result. People with PD are unable to control their body movements. This results in the characteristic signs of tremors (shaking) in the arms and legs, stiff muscles, shuffling gait, trouble with small movements such as writing, or with larger movements such as standing up and walking.

Dopamine is so important to so many body functions that even a minor imbalance in its levels in the brain can cause significant issues. It is responsible for much of what makes human beings behave the way they do. As psychiatrist Emily Deans says:

> We need dopamine in the right place at the right time in the right amounts. When it all comes together, we are the awesomest ape around. Dopamine will motivate us, and it is the driving neurotransmitter in competitive behaviors. When

our dopamine machinery isn't working properly, problems ensue (not surprisingly). Dopamine is linked to everything interesting about metabolism, evolution, and the brain.[6]

What Happens in Parkinson's Disease?

PD develops when dopaminergic neurons in the substantia nigra begin to die off. No one knows for certain why this happens or what causes it to start. In autopsies (examinations of

An illustration shows the substantia nigra (black area in the inset) part of the brain. Parkinson's causes the loss of neurons in the substantia nigra, which affects motor abilities.

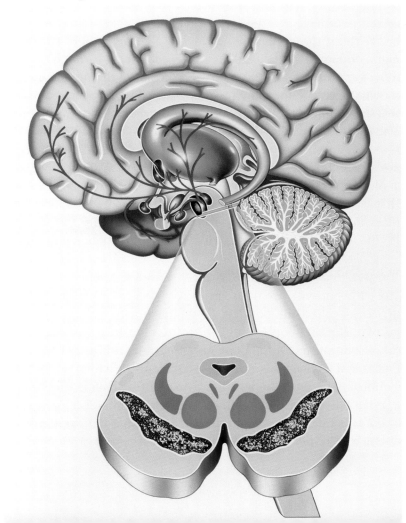

the body after death), the brain of PD patients may appear normal, but on closer examination of the substantia nigra, definite changes can be seen. First, its neurons appear to have lost the dark pigment that gives the structure its name. There are far fewer of them than in a healthy brain, and the ones that remain show signs of deformity. They also contain small dark specks called Lewy bodies. Lewy bodies are abnormal collections of a protein called alpha-synuclein (alfa sin-NU-klee-in). Lewy bodies also appear in other neurological disorders besides PD, such as Alzheimer's disease and Lewy body dementia.

At first, other parts of the brain that contain dopaminergic neurons are able to make up for the loss of neurons in the substantia nigra. Eventually, however, when about 50 to 70 percent of the neurons have died, the symptoms of PD begin to show up. Without the dopamine-producing neurons of the substantia nigra, dopamine is lost, and messages cannot get through to other movement centers in the brain. The result is the appearance of the characteristic movement symptoms of PD. To make matters worse, as dopamine is lost, other neurotransmitters in the brain also decline, which leads to other kinds of PD symptoms such as depression and anxiety. "These neurotransmitter and cell changes are spread widely throughout the brain," says William J. Weiner, a physician and former director of the Maryland Parkinson's Disease Center, "which may help explain why dopamine replacement does not correct all the problems caused by Parkinson's. . . . In short, Parkinson's is not just a dopamine deficiency state."[7]

Young-Onset Parkinson's Disease

Most PD patients are over age sixty. This more common form of PD is called idiopathic PD, which means its cause is not known. Not all people who get PD are elderly, however. Sometimes symptoms can appear much earlier in life. Young-onset Parkinson's disease (YOPD) is diagnosed when a person's symptoms begin to appear before age fifty. This is the kind of PD that astronaut Rich Clifford and actor Michael J. Fox developed. It is much less common than idiopathic PD, appearing in about 5 to 10 percent of PD patients.

How the Brain Tracks Time

One of the more important of the brain's many functions is tracking time, and this is more complicated than simply knowing what time it is or how long an hour is. Encoding time is necessary for carrying out a multitude of daily tasks such as walking up stairs or clapping in time to music. A sense of timing is needed in order to perform a series of actions, such as taking one step after another while walking. Normally, people do not have to think much about walking. In some patients with Parkinson's, however, it is thought that the "timing circuit" in the brain is impaired. Timing cannot occur naturally, so much more conscious thought is required to perform the activity.

In 2009 a team of neuroscientists at the Massachusetts Institute of Technology discovered some important information about how brain cells keep track of time. Using specially designed electrodes, the researchers were able to study the function of specific neurons in the basal ganglia (which includes the substantia nigra, the area associated with PD) of macaque monkeys who were taught to perform a simple timing task. They learned that some neurons did not do any real "thinking," but instead simply provided "ticks" for other neurons to "listen to" so they could track timing. The timing neurons fired at specific intervals, measured in milliseconds (thousandths of a second). The research is important for PD patients because it provides a way to detect and measure neuron activity as fast as it occurs, paving the way for potential new treatments that target the activity.

Another major difference between YOPD and idiopathic PD is that it seems to be associated with genetic mutations, or abnormalities. PD is not usually considered a genetic disease and does not tend to run in families, but as many as 50 percent of YOPD patients may have a gene mutation linked to PD.

YOPD has been associated with abnormal versions of certain genes with names such as PARK2, PARK9, DJ-I, and PINK1. In 1998 the PARK2 gene, which codes for a protein called parkin, became the first of these genes to be associated with PD, and it is the most common mutation associated with YOPD. The function of the parkin protein in the body is not clearly known, but the main theory is that it helps degrade other proteins that are toxic to dopaminergic neurons. The PARK2 mutation is a recessive trait, which means that a person must inherit a copy of the defective gene from each parent in order for YOPD symptoms to develop. Another distinguishing feature is that YOPD patients who have the PARK2 mutation do not develop Lewy bodies in their brains.

The symptoms of YOPD are similar to those of idiopathic PD, but there are some differences. For example, YOPD tends to progress more slowly than idiopathic PD, and younger patients are less likely to develop PD-related dementia. Younger patients may have a higher incidence of dystonias, which are involuntary muscle contractions that can force body parts (in YOPD, most commonly the feet) into abnormal and sometimes painful positions. For unknown reasons, younger patients tend to be more sensitive to small doses of the most effective treatment drug, levodopa, and may develop certain side effects of medication sooner after starting treatment than older patients. Treatment for YOPD is similar, although the long-term use of PD medications is of greater concern for younger patients; some undesirable side effects of long-term PD medications may show up while these patients are still working and raising families.

Juvenile-Onset Parkinsonism

At age fifteen, Paola was a normal teenage girl, dealing with normal teenage things like friends and school. Then everything changed. "I was only 12 years old when everything started," she says. "I didn't pay attention to those things until one afternoon I was doing my math homework and my hand started to shake. I couldn't write a single number in the paper. That was the first time I felt helpless."[8] She had no idea what was going on.

Her grandfather had been seeing a neurologist for Parkinson's disease, so Paola went to see the same doctor. She explains:

> After I had a lot of tests . . . the doctor diagnosed me with PD. It was very difficult for my family and for me to believe it. We did a lot of research, and we weren't able to find another person of my age who had PD. I was only a little girl. I was really scared, especially when I thought about my grandfather. He spent most of the time in bed, unable to move, talk or eat by himself. I tried to live like a normal girl and do the same things as my friends with the only difference that I had to take pills three times a day. None of my friends knew about my PD because I could hide my symptoms very well.[9]

Very rarely, a person may develop Parkinson-like symptoms before age twenty. This is called juvenile-onset parkinsonism. Unlike idiopathic PD and YOPD, it is almost always a genetic illness and is actually considered a different disease. For this reason, it is usually referred to as a form of parkinsonism, rather than a true form of Parkinson's disease. Its symptoms also follow a different course than PD. For example, the muscle cramping of dystonia is even more common in juvenile-onset parkinsonism than in YOPD. There may also be seizures, visual problems, lack of coordination of movement (called ataxia), and problems with thinking processes such as learning and remembering. Juvenile-onset parkinsonism may go undetected for many years because it is so uncommon; there may be many causes for the symptoms, and children and teens may try to hide the symptoms from others. Today Paola is married and the mother of a healthy son. She has not allowed her condition to stop her from enjoying life fully. "It has been 16 years now," she says, "and every day I wake up I wonder how my day is going to be, if I will have off episodes or maybe not. Today is what we have, and we have to make the most of it."[10]

CHAPTER TWO

Causes and Symptoms

Almost two hundred years after James Parkinson's ground-breaking essay, Parkinson's disease remains a mystery to the scientists who study it, the doctors who treat it, and the patients and families who live with it. William J. Weiner explains:

> As of now, we don't know why one person develops Parkinson's and another does not. Science and medicine have told us some things about Parkinson's, but we still have much to learn. For example, although Parkinson's appears to be one of the most common neurodegenerative diseases in the United States and Canada, even after extensive studies we don't know for sure how many people have it, or who will get it, or why.[11]

One of the major reasons Parkinson's disease is such a mystery is that, like most neurodegenerative diseases, its exact causes are largely unknown. This is why the most common form of PD—the one that affects older people—is often referred to as "idiopathic" Parkinson's, which means "of unknown cause." Although scientists know what happens in the brain of PD patients to cause the symptoms (the death of dopamine-producing neurons in the substantia nigra portion of the brain), it is not clear what causes the die-off to occur in the first place. There are several theories, but no solid answers.

Inside and Outside

The cause of most diseases or disorders falls into one of two major categories—genetic or environmental. Genetic diseases are those that are caused by mutations, or abnormalities, in one or more genes. Some genetic diseases are passed from parent to child and can run in families, such as sickle-cell anemia, cystic fibrosis, and hemophilia. Others are caused by a spontaneous mutation that is not passed from parent to child but happens for unknown reasons, such as Down syndrome. There is some scientific evidence that PD may have a genetic component to it. About 20 percent of people with PD have a close family member who also has it. However, this does not necessarily mean that having a family history of PD increases a person's risk; most people with PD do not know of anyone else in their family who has had it. Family history does seem to be more of a risk factor, however, in the juvenile-onset and early onset forms of PD, because they are more commonly associated with genetic mutations.

Environmental diseases are those that are caused by something that comes from outside the person, such as pathogens (viruses, parasites, bacteria, and so forth) or chemicals and toxins (cigarette smoke, alcohol, drugs, pollution, and so forth). Studies looking for environmental causes for PD have suggested that long-term exposure to herbicides and pesticides used in farming may contribute to developing PD later in life. Other environmental factors that may be linked to PD include exposure to certain solvent chemicals, lower caffeine consumption, and smoking. As with genetic causes, however, environmental factors are not certain causes. For example, it is uncommon for both a husband and wife to get PD, even if they live together for a long time and are exposed to the same environmental influences.

It is possible that PD may be a result of a combination of both genetic and environmental factors. Some people may have a genetic predisposition to PD—a genetic makeup that makes it easier for them to develop PD if they are exposed to one of the potential environmental triggers such as a pesticide. Other people may have a genetic structure that actually protects them from PD. These individuals, if exposed to an environmental trigger, may be less likely to get PD.

Oxidative Stress

A third possible cause that has been getting a lot of recent scientific attention is called oxidative stress (OS). OS is a normal biological process that occurs constantly inside cells, at the molecular level, and causes cell damage over the course of a person's life. OS is linked to the aging process and age-related diseases such as cancer and heart disease, and to neurodegenerative diseases such as Alzheimer's and Parkinson's. OS occurs when molecules in the cells become unstable and try to restabilize themselves.

All the cells of the body are made up of molecules, which in turn are made up of atoms. Atoms consist of a central core called the nucleus. The nucleus is made of tiny particles called protons and neutrons. Other particles called electrons orbit the nucleus similarly to the way the moon orbits the earth. An

Oxidative stress granules, more commonly known as free radicals, are shown here in white occurring in a cancer cell. They are produced when cells metabolize oxygen.

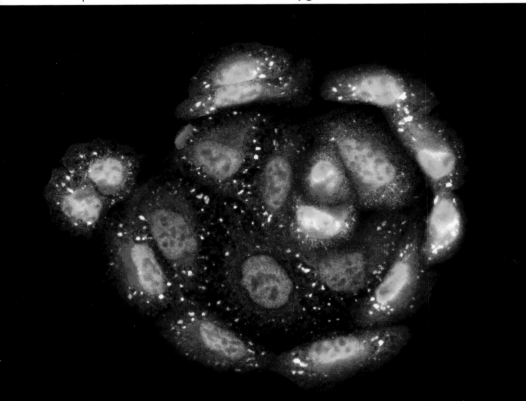

atom that contains the same number of protons and electrons is stable and tends not to react with other atoms. Atoms seek stability, so if an atom is lacking one or more electrons, it will try to become stable by forming a chemical bond with another atom in order to "share" electrons.

If the chemical bond between atoms in a molecule splits, unstable molecules called free radicals are formed. In their quest to become stable, free radicals may "attack" a nearby molecule and attempt to take an electron for themselves. When this happens, the second molecule also becomes a free radical, and a chain reaction is started. After a while, the entire cell (such as a neuron in the brain) can be disrupted by this chain reaction of unstable molecules stealing electrons from stable molecules, and the cell cannot function normally. This chain reaction is what causes oxidative stress in the cell.

Usually, free radicals can be repaired by substances in the body called antioxidants. Antioxidants are stable molecules that remain stable even if they lose an electron. Vitamins C and E are examples of antioxidants. However, outside factors such as pollution, radiation, toxic chemicals, and cigarette smoke can cause an increased production of free radicals. If there are not enough antioxidants in the body to repair them, the process of oxidative stress is speeded up, and cellular damage results. The damage builds up with age and leads to cell death. The theory is that if this occurs in dopamine-producing neurons, it may contribute to the development of PD.

Hallmark Symptoms of Parkinson's Disease

It is not only the lack of clear cause that makes PD a mystery, but also its lack of clear-cut symptoms. There are dozens of different signs and symptoms associated with PD. One person may have one set of symptoms, and another person may have a completely different set. Symptoms may be more severe in one person than in another, and they may appear in a different order or at a different time in the course of the disease. Even in the same person, they may appear and disappear, or they may be mild one day and more severe the next. They begin gradually and may go unnoticed by other people and even by the person who has them. Often they are dismissed as just a normal part of aging. "So slight and nearly imperceptible are the first inroads of this malady," wrote James Parkinson, "and so extremely slow its progress, that it rarely happens, that the patient can form any recollection of the precise period of its commencement."[12]

This was true for Frankie Miller's grandfather, for whom she is named. Miller explains:

> At first the symptoms were small and not that noticeable, my mother told him it is probably arthritis from working in a factory with his hands for so many years. As months went by though we started to notice my grandfather slowing down, but he'd say it was just arthritis. Finally, my grandfather agreed to go to a place in New Haven that specializes in Parkinson's Research. Sadly, the brain scan showed signs of Parkinson's.[13]

PD has four hallmark symptoms that appear in almost all people affected by the disease. These main signs are sometimes referred to by the acronym *TRAP*. The *T* stands for "tremor." One of the earliest and most common signs, appearing in about 75 percent of patients, tremor involves the involuntary or uncontrollable shaking of a smaller body part such as a finger, hand, arm, or less commonly, the chin or lip. It usually begins on one side and can stay on that side for years. Later in the illness, tremors appear in other areas, such as the leg, but almost always on the same side as the initial tremor. The tremors are generally resting tremors; they tend to appear when the affected part is at rest and subside when the person moves that part of the body. They tend to get worse when the patient is feeling any kind of strong emotion, and lessen when the patient is calm again. They also subside while the person is asleep and resume a few minutes after waking up. Some patients may have tremors that do not show on the outside, but the person feels as if the muscles of the arms, legs, or abdomen are trembling on the inside.

Is There a Parkinsonian Personality?

Since the early 1900s physicians who treat PD patients, and family members who live with them, have noticed that there seems to be a so-called parkinsonian personality. Many believe that people with PD tend to have certain personality traits that have been in place for years before the disease makes its first appearance. According to this observation, people who develop PD tend to follow rules strictly. They are serious, punctual, and cautious people who tend to avoid taking risks. They tend to be introverted and slow to show temper. This correlation between PD and personality has to do with dopamine. Writes Patrick Mc-Namara, Director of the Evolutionary Neurobehavior Laboratory in the Department of Neurology at Boston University:

> The idea is that loss of dopamine starts years before any movement problems emerge and this loss of dopamine has subtle effects on the personality. Given that dopamine is the brain chemical that allows you to feel energy, pleasure, and thrills, it follows that if you are low on dopamine, you may become more introverted and less willing to take risks for a cheap thrill. Interestingly, persons with PD tend not to smoke or to engage in other risky health behaviors.

> Certain medications for PD, however, can reverse these personality traits in the patient because they stimulate the limbic system, the part of the brain that regulates emotion and thrill seeking. PD patients on these medications, called dopamine agonists, may begin to engage in risk-taking behaviors and may therefore need more supervision.

Patrick McNamara, "Is There a Parkinsonian Personality?" About.com, May 9, 2009. http://parkinsons.about.com/od/faqs/f/parinsons_personality.htm.

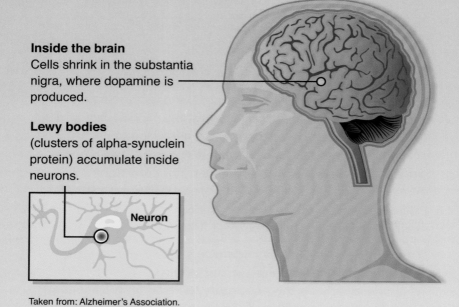

Parkinson's Symptoms

Cognitive: Loss of executive functions, including planning, decision making, and controlling emotions.

Physical: Tremors, stiffness, and slowed movements.

Inside the brain
Cells shrink in the substantia nigra, where dopamine is produced.

Lewy bodies
(clusters of alpha-synuclein protein) accumulate inside neurons.

Neuron

Taken from: Alzheimer's Association.

The *R* stands for "rigidity." The muscles of the arms, legs, neck, back, or trunk feel stiff, inflexible, and painful. For about 10 percent of patients, such as astronaut Rich Clifford, an early sign of muscle rigidity is a stiff shoulder, called frozen shoulder. Others may feel as though one leg is dragging, and they may appear to walk with a limp. There are two types of muscle rigidity associated with PD, which the doctor may find when examining a patient's joints and muscles. One is known as lead pipe rigidity. This is a smooth resistance to being moved, like the feeling of bending a soft lead pipe. The other is known as cogwheel rigidity. This resistance feels jerky or ratchet-like to the doctor moving the affected part of the body.

The *A* stands for "akinesia." *Akinesia* means "absence of movement." This sign may also be called bradykinesia, which means "slow movement." People with PD tend to move slowly and with small, limited movements. They walk very slowly, with small, shuffling steps, and tend to adopt a stooped or bent-over posture when standing, due to rigidity in the abdominal muscles. They may have trouble beginning to walk, or they may suddenly stop and not be able to resume walking, as

Trembling hands of a person suffering from Parkinson's disease attempting to thread a needle.

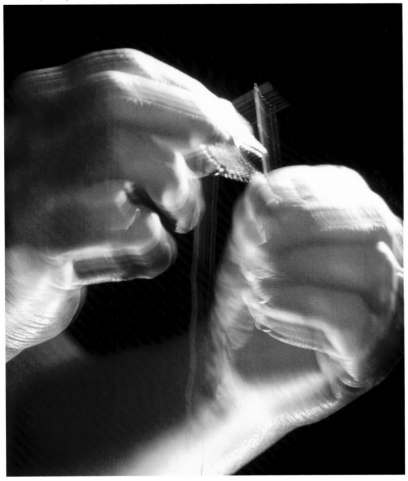

if their feet were stuck to the floor. This is called motor block, or freezing, and tends to happen when a person turns around, changes direction, or passes through a narrow doorway. Akinesia can also cause problems when a person has been in a resting position, such as in a chair or in bed, and tries to get up or turn over. Getting out of a car can also be very difficult.

The *P* stands for "postural instability." This means difficulty maintaining balance when standing or walking. It is caused by an impairment in the set of reflexes needed for maintaining balance. People with PD may feel unsteady on their feet. They may have trouble turning around without losing balance. They may tend to lean—forward, backward, or sideways. Later in the progression of the disease, they may lose their balance often and fall very easily, especially if they try to turn quickly, if they walk on an uneven surface, or if someone bumps into them. Other times they may fall for no apparent reason whatsoever.

Stages of Parkinson's Disease

The TRAP symptoms of PD are the most common symptoms, but they are not by any means the only symptoms. Many other symptoms may arise as the disease progresses. PD tends to progress over the years in stages. James Parkinson recognized the progressive nature of PD in his patients. He wrote:

> The first symptoms perceived are, a slight sense of weakness, with a proneness to trembling in some particular part; sometimes in the head, but most commonly in one of the hands and arms. After a few more months the patient is found to be less strict than usual in preserving an upright posture: this being most observable whilst walking, but sometimes whilst sitting or standing. Walking becomes a task which cannot be performed without considerable attention. . . . At this period the patient experiences much inconvenience, which unhappily is found daily to increase. As time and the disease proceed, difficulties increase: writing can now be hardly at all accomplished; and reading, from the tremulous motion, is accomplished with some difficulty.[14]

Some care providers divide PD progression into five stages, called the Hoehn and Yahr rating scale, developed in 1967. Another method describes its progression in terms of early, moderate, and advanced-stage PD. Like other characteristics of PD, the stages may not occur in the same order from person to person; they may vary in length or include different sets of symptoms, and sometimes a stage might even be skipped entirely.

Early Parkinson's Disease

The early stage of PD includes stage 1 of the Hoehn and Yahr scale. In stage 1 of PD, most people experience milder symptoms that may be annoying but do not yet interfere very much with activities of daily living. Many early symptoms have to do with muscle movement and function. People may notice mild

Running in the Family

A form of Parkinson's that is clearly genetic (called "familial" Parkinson's) has been identified in a small number of families living in France, the United States, Canada, Ireland, and Italy. A team of international researchers at the Mayo Clinic in Jacksonville, Florida, has studied the genetics of these families. In 2011 the team reported the discovery of a gene that is present in the family members. The gene, named EIF4G1, seems to be related to the ability of the body's cells to deal with stress by governing the manufacture of certain proteins that protect cells from stress, such as aging. Mutations (genetic "mistakes") in this gene, which get passed from parent to child in the families who have it, leave cells, including brain cells, unable to adapt to the normal stresses of aging. EIF4G1 is the third gene discovered by this team of researchers that appears to contribute to Parkinson's disease. The researchers believe that genes that contribute to familial PD may also play a role in the more typical form of the disease. The identification of these genes may lead to new therapies to treat PD or at least slow its progression.

tremors in one limb and on one side of the body. They may notice that they have lost some coordination in their hands and feel clumsy when trying to type, fasten buttons, or write. A common sign of PD is micrographia, which means "small writing," in which the person's handwriting becomes very small and hard to read. They may experience foot cramps in the morning, which may or may not be painful. Changes in the voice may occur; the person may feel as if his or her voice has lost strength and that he or she cannot speak loudly or clearly. The person may speak in a monotone, with little or none of the normal variations in pitch.

People in early PD may report vague symptoms such as fatigue, weakness, trouble sleeping, and general aches and pains in the upper body, including frozen shoulder. They may have sensory symptoms such as numbness and tingling, a burning sensation in the skin, and feelings of heat or cold in their limbs, back, neck, and abdomen. A common early sensory sign is a decreased sense of smell, which affects how food tastes to the PD patient.

Moderate Parkinson's Disease

The progression from stage 1 to stage 2 can take years to occur, and there is no way to predict how the disease will progress in any individual person. In stage 2 the symptoms of stage 1 become more noticeable. The tremors begin to show up in other limbs or on the other side of the body, and muscle stiffness becomes more noticeable. The muscle rigidity and bradykinesia of PD may also show in the face; other people may notice that the person does not seem to show much facial expression and seems to be staring all the time. This is called masked expression, or masking, and is common in early or moderate PD. Walking becomes slower and more difficult, and the person may begin to develop the characteristic stooped-over posture and shuffling gait of PD. Balance, however, is not yet impaired in stage 2. Basic activities become more difficult, such as getting out of bed or up from a chair, and fatigue becomes worse as sleep problems arise.

This Parkinson's patient shows symptoms of facial muscle stiffness called masking. Masking is usually seen in PD patients who have progressed to stage 2 on the Hoehn and Yahr scale.

At this stage cognitive and emotional changes may become more apparent. Cognitive processes include mental skills such as memory, concentration, attention, learning, problem solving, logic, reasoning, and interpreting visual and auditory information. PD patients may struggle with slow thinking, trouble finding the right word, and difficulty paying attention or making decisions.

Mood disorders such as depression and anxiety related to the diagnosis of PD may show up, especially in younger patients who are still in their working years. As many as 50 percent of PD patients experience some degree of depression. Depression is more than just "having the blues." Depression is a persistent and life-affecting disorder of mood involving feelings of sadness and hopelessness. It tends to be worse if cognitive problems are also present, and depression can in turn make cognitive problems worse. Anxiety is a normal human emotion that everyone feels from time to time, such as before a big test, an audition, or an important meeting. Chronic (long-term) anxiety, however, is a mood disorder that can seriously affect a person's quality of life. Anxiety causes a person to view the world with fear, worry, doubt, and sometimes panic. It can cause physical symptoms such as shortness of breath, stomach upset, rapid heartbeat, or skin rashes. Like depression, anxiety can make cognitive issues worse, and vice versa.

Stage 3 is considered to be a turning point in the progression of PD. A person is considered to be in stage 3 when there is significant slowing of muscle movement. Maintaining balance and equilibrium is now more difficult, reflexes are diminished, and walking in a straight line is a challenge. In stage 3 the symptoms begin to make a major impact on the person's ability to perform activities of daily living, although the person is still able to complete most of them without much help.

Advanced Parkinson's Disease

The main difference between stage 3 and stage 4 of PD is in independence. The person may still be able to walk but may require the use of a walker, motorized chair, or other assistive device. Freezing may become more frequent. Reaction time is significantly slowed, and some daily activities such as getting out of bed or up from a chair or preparing a meal are now almost impossible to complete without help. Driving is usually impossible for someone at this stage. Most patients in stage 4 can no longer live on their own. For reasons that are not fully understood, the tremors and shaking that characterized the earlier stages may now lessen or even stop completely.

Stage 5 is the final and most debilitating stage of PD. In stage 5 the person may no longer be able to stand or walk, even with help, and may require a wheelchair to get around. People in stage 5 can do very little for themselves and require care and supervision around the clock. Psychological symptoms such as hallucinations and delusions may occur. Eventually, these individuals become completely dependent on others for all their care. They can no longer swallow or control bowel or bladder function. At this stage the side effects of medications may outweigh any benefit they provide.

Persons with advanced Parkinson's disease may require the use of a walker, motorized chair, or other assistive device to get around.

Pain and Parkinson's Disease

One of the issues for many patients dealing with Parkinson's disease is pain. Sensory signals can be impaired in PD, and many PD patients experience sensory symptoms such as vision problems or a loss of taste or smell. Pain is also a sensory issue, and there are several types of pain associated with PD. Musculoskeletal pain from muscle stiffness and rigidity is the most common kind of pain for PD patients. It may begin one to two years before movement symptoms such as tremors appear. A common cause is frozen shoulder, but patients may also experience musculoskeletal pain in the back, neck, and hips. Radiculopathy is a kind of pain that occurs close to a nerve. Patients describe this as a kind of shooting pain that goes down the length of an arm or leg. A common kind of radiculopathy in PD is sciatica—pain or tingling that goes down the back of the leg. A third kind of pain is dystonia, which is the prolonged and involuntary spasm, or cramping, of one or more muscles. PD patients, especially young-onset PD patients, commonly get dystonia in their feet and toes, but dystonic cramps can also occur in the neck, face, or jaw. Other sources of pain for PD patients may be burning or stinging sensations in various parts of the body, headaches, or restless legs syndrome.

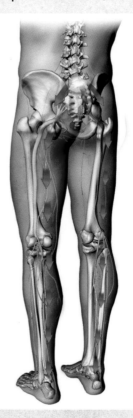

Radiculopathy is often felt as a shooting pain down the leg.

The Unified Parkinson's Disease Rating Scale

Some care providers for PD patients do not use the Hoehn and Yahr scale because it focuses mainly on the physical and movement symptoms of PD, and there are many other signs and symptoms of PD that are not movement related. The Unified Parkinson's Disease Rating Scale (UPDRS) is another scale that measures progression of PD so that treatment decisions can be made. It includes a modified form of the Hoehn and Yahr scale, along with another scale called the Schwab and England scale, which assesses ability to perform activities of daily living. The UPDRS also includes evaluation of mental, emotional, and behavioral signs. This very detailed and comprehensive five-part assessment tool addresses forty-two points, including things such as intellectual impairment, motivation and initiative, speech, swallowing, handwriting, dressing, hygiene, falling, freezing, tremors, speech, facial expression, posture, gait, complications of therapy, sleep disturbances, and many others.

Scales such as the Hoehn and Yahr and the UPDRS can be helpful in evaluating a person's progression through PD and can help in making treatment decisions. But even the codeveloper of Hoehn and Yahr, Margaret M. Hoehn, acknowledges the limitations of these scales due to the unpredictable nature of PD. She writes:

> For example, while general experience has been that it is the onset of disturbances of balance that heralds future disability, some patients may have such severe tremor that they are incapacitated even though balance is intact. Others may have mild disturbance of balance for many years without losing independence. There are occasional patients who are more incapacitated by severe unilateral [one-sided] disease than are others by milder bilateral [both sides] disease. Sometimes Stage 1 is skipped and the onset is bilateral or generalized. Similarly, many patients never reach Stage 5. The scale is not linear; that is, the patient does not remain at each stage for the same number of years; nor does any stage necessarily represent a given amount of [disease] in the brain.[15]

Unified Parkinson's Disease Rating Scale

I. Mentation, Behavior and Mood

1. Intellectual Impairment

0 = None.
1 = Mild. Consistent forgetfulness with partial recollection of events and no other difficulties.
2 = Moderate memory loss, with disorientation and moderate difficulty handling complex problems. Mild but definite impairment of function at home with need of occasional prompting.
3 = Severe memory loss with disorientation for time and often to place. Severe impairment in handling problems.
4 = Severe memory loss with orientation preserved to person only. Unable to make judgements or solve problems. Requires much help with personal care. Cannot be left alone at all.

2. Thought Disorder

0 = None.
1 = Vivid dreaming.
2 = "Benign" hallucinations with insight retained.
3 = Occasional to frequent hallucinations or delusions; without insight; could interfere with daily activities.
4 = Persistent hallucinations, delusions, or florrid psychosis. Not able to care for self.

3. Depression

1 = Periods of sadness or guilt greater than normal, never sustained for days or weeks.
2 = Sustained depression (1 week or more).
3 = Sustained depression with vegetative symptoms (insomnia, anorexia, weight loss, loss of interest).
4 = Sustained depression with vegetative symptoms and suicidal thoughts or intent.

4. Motivation/Initiative

0 = Normal.
1 = Less assertive than usual; more passive.
2 = Loss of initiative or disinterest in elective (non-routine) activities.
3 = Loss of initiative or disinterest in day to day (routine) activities.
4 = Withdrawn, complete loss of motivation.

II. Activities of Daily Living (for both "on" and off")

5. Speech

0 = Normal.
1 = Mildly affected. No difficulty being understood.
2 = Moderately affected. Sometimes asked to repeat statements.
3 = Severely affected. Frequently asked to repeat statements.
4 = Unintelligible most of the time.

6. Salivation

0 = Normal.
1 = Slight but definite excess of saliva in mouth, may have some nighttime drooling.
2 = Moderately excessive saliva; may have minimal drooling.
3 = Marked excess of saliva with some drooling.
4 = Marked drooling, requires constant tissue or handkerchief.

7. Swallowing

0 = Normal.
1 = Rare choking.
2 = Occasional choking.
3 = Requires soft food.
4 = Requires NG tube or gastrotomy feeding.

Taken from: The We Move Clinicians Guide to Parkinson's Disease. © We Move 2006.

The relative lack of knowledge about what causes PD, the wide variety of its symptoms, and the unpredictable occurrence and progression of symptoms from person to person can make the diagnosis and treatment of PD extremely difficult. Contributing to the difficulty are the many other conditions that can cause similar symptoms.

CHAPTER THREE

Diagnosis of Parkinson's Disease

David Dalton was only forty-four years old in 1994 when he and his wife, Patsy, went to their doctor to find out what was causing his muscle stiffness and loss of coordination in his hands. At the time, they were told that it could be Parkinson's disease but that it could also be thyroid problems or a brain tumor. When the other two possibilities were ruled out, PD was diagnosed. The Daltons did not understand the diagnosis at first. Like most people, they had thought of PD as a disease of older people with shaky hands. He was not having any tremors, and he was young. "We went home and looked it up in the dictionary," says David, "and it said 'progressive nervous disorder.' The word 'progressive' seemed to be in much larger print than 'nervous disorder,' even though they were all the same size. It just jumped out at you."[16]

The Daltons' confusion was understandable. Parkinson's disease is just one of several medical conditions that show similar symptoms and can look like Parkinson's disease. Symptoms such as tremors, muscle stiffness, slow movements, loss of balance, trouble speaking and swallowing, and problems with memory and thought processes may also be caused by other conditions that are not Parkinson's disease. Several other conditions that cause similar symptoms as PD are grouped into a category of illnesses called atypical parkinsonism, or Parkinson-plus syndromes. Most of these include some symptoms that do not appear in PD, as well as those that do. This can make the diagnosis and treatment of PD confusing and difficult.

Essential Tremor

Essential tremor is the most common movement disorder; it affects more than 5 million people in the United States. It can affect people of any age, although it is most common in those over age fifty. The typical cause in about half of all cases is an inherited genetic mutation. This is called a familial tremor. In cases that are not inherited from a parent, the cause is unknown. The tremors of essential tremor may be mild, moderate, or severe. They begin gradually but can worsen over time. They most often involve the hands, head, and voice and are rarely seen in the lower body.

Essential tremor may look like early-stage PD, but it is different from PD in that the tremors show on both sides from the beginning. In addition, PD tremors are noticeable when the arms are at rest, but the tremors of essential tremor become more noticeable when the person tries to do something with his or her hands, such as eat soup with a spoon or pick up a cup of coffee. Drugs used to treat PD are not effective for essential tremor because the cause of the disorder is not the same.

Vascular Parkinsonism

Vascular parkinsonism, also called multi-infarct parkinsonism, is caused by impaired blood flow to the brain due to multiple small strokes. An infarct is an interruption in blood flow caused by a blood clot inside a blood vessel, and when this happens repeatedly in the vessels that carry blood to the brain, damage to the brain can result. The most common causes of vascular parkinsonism are long-term hypertension (high blood pressure) and diabetes. Other causes include heart disease or a blockage in the carotid arteries, which carry blood to the brain. Both of these can cause blood clots in the arteries to break off and travel to the brain, where they can become lodged in the small arteries there.

Symptoms of vascular parkinsonism can include trouble with speaking, swallowing, or moving the muscles of the face. It can cause problems with confusion, thinking processes, and

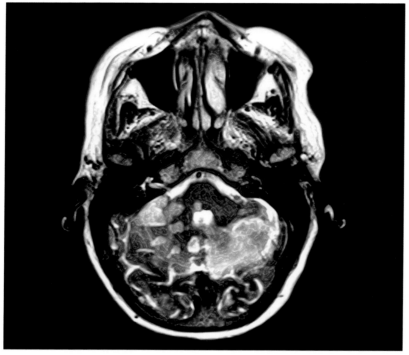

An MRI of a cerebellum (back part of a brain) shows infarctions, seen as white areas in the blue, lower part of the image.

control of bowel or bladder function (incontinence). Tremor is not as common. Like PD, the symptoms of vascular parkinsonism progress over time. Medications used to treat PD may be used, but they may not be effective because, like essential tremor, the cause is not the same as for PD.

Drugs and Chemicals

Certain drugs used for treating mental illnesses such as schizophrenia can block the actions of dopamine and cause parkinsonism. Other drugs used for stomach disorders or high blood pressure can also cause the symptoms. The major differences between drug-induced parkinsonism and PD are that the symptoms, once begun, do not change much over time, and it is reversible; if the person stops taking the drug, the parkinsonian symptoms will subside.

Toxic chemicals in a person's environment can also cause parkinsonism. Examples include manganese dust (formed during stainless-steel manufacture), carbon monoxide (found in engine exhaust fumes and cigarette smoke), and carbon disulfide (a poisonous liquid used in rubber and paint removers, and as a solvent for oils). In the 1980s a chemical called MPTP was found to cause a permanent form of parkinsonism in heroin addicts who had used drugs contaminated with the chemical. Scientists at the time used this information to simulate PD in lab animals in order to learn more about it.

Toxic chemicals in a person's environment, such as paint remover and other solvents, have been linked to Parkinson's.

Other Neurological Causes of Parkinsonism

Several other neurological conditions can cause symptoms of parkinsonism. Lewy body dementia is a brain disorder with symptoms that are similar to both PD and Alzheimer's disease. It is caused by the buildup of abnormal proteins called Lewy bodies in the neurons of the brain. Damage to dopaminergic neurons in Lewy body dementia causes motor symptoms simi-

Professional Athletes and Parkinsonism

Muhammad Ali is possibly the best-known professional boxer of all time. His slogan during his fighting career was "Float like a butterfly, sting like a bee." Today, however, it is clear that something is very wrong. At age seventy-two, the three-time world heavyweight champion can barely speak or walk, and his hands and arms tremble constantly. In 1984, when his symptoms first became noticeable, he went through extensive testing at several major medical centers. A number of brain abnormalities were discovered, all of which were thought to be related to the repeated blows to the head that he sustained over his long boxing career. Most significantly, his brain stem, in which many dopamine-producing neurons are located, was seriously damaged. At only forty-two years of age, he was diagnosed with parkinsonism related to head trauma.

Head injuries, especially if they are severe or repeated over time, can cause a form of parkinsonism. The kind of parkinsonism that affected Ali is called dementia pugilistica, commonly referred to as being "punch drunk." It is often seen in boxers who sustain repeated blows to the head over the course of their careers. It is also thought to affect professional football players, who may experience many blows to the head and multiple concussions. When

lar to PD. People with this disorder may have problems with memory, concentration, and attention. They may have difficulty expressing their thoughts with words or planning things in the future. Hallucinations are common. They may be unable to do simple tasks such as tying their shoes or combing their hair. They may have parkinsonian symptoms such as tremors, slow movement, shuffling gait, muscle stiffness, masked facial expression, and difficulties with speech and swallowing. Like PD, Lewy body dementia is progressive, and there is no cure.

Football Hall of Famer Forrest Gregg was diagnosed with parkinsonism, his neurologist, an expert in movement disorders, said that his many concussions may have triggered his disease. A 2012 study of retired NFL players by the Centers for Disease Control and Prevention concluded that professional football players are three times more likely than other athletes to develop neurodegenerative diseases. The study led to new rules for football players at all levels about helmet use and playing time after a head injury.

Former world heavyweight boxing champion Muhammad Ali is the world's most recognizable sufferer of parkinsonism. His long career in boxing is the probable cause.

Progressive supranuclear palsy (PSP) is a common form of atypical parkinsonism. Like Lewy body dementia, it is caused by the buildup of abnormal proteins in the brain, but in PSP, the proteins are called tau proteins. Like PD, the symptoms usually begin after age fifty, but they progress faster than in PD. Symptoms include problems with balance and falling, muscle rigidity, and speech and swallowing problems. PSP patients eventually lose the ability to move their eyes up and down, and later in the illness, dementia develops.

Multiple-system atrophy (MSA), formerly called Shy-Drager syndrome, is a neurodegenerative disorder that causes one or more parts of the autonomic nervous system to fail. The autonomic nervous system is the part of the nervous system that controls involuntary functions such as heart rate, breathing, blood pressure, and intestinal function. It also controls skin and body temperature and is involved in the body's reactions to stress. The cause of MSA is not known for certain, but examination of brain tissue after death shows shrinkage in portions of the brain that control these functions, as well as a buildup of alpha-synuclein protein in the neurons. MSA usually begins during a person's fifties and can cause fainting spells and problems with heart rate or bladder control. It includes parkinsonian symptoms such as tremor, slow movement, muscle rigidity, poor balance, and lack of coordination of muscle movements. Symptoms progress faster than in PD, and it does not respond to drugs used to treat PD.

Corticobasal degeneration (CBD) is an uncommon form of parkinsonism that develops usually in a person's sixties and also progresses faster than PD. It is caused by loss of neurons and shrinkage of several areas of the brain, including the substantia nigra. Like other disorders of parkinsonism, it can cause muscle rigidity, slow movement, muscle spasms, language problems, and eventually, inability to walk. PD drugs are also not helpful for CBD.

Diagnosing Parkinson's Disease

One of the greatest challenges for health-care professionals attempting to make an accurate diagnosis for a person with

Dopamine Transporter Imaging

Some types of positron emission tomography (PET) scans, as well as another imaging test called single-photon emission computed tomography, or SPECT, have been used for some time in Europe, and since 2011 in North America, to specifically look at the dopamine-producing system in the brain. These scans, while not valuable in distinguishing PD from most other forms of parkinsonism, can distinguish between essential tremor and PD. This helps eliminate a very common cause of tremors from the list of possible causes.

Dopamine works as a neurotransmitter by carrying electrical messages from one neuron to the next across the synapse, or gap, between the neurons. After the message is carried across the synapse, the dopamine is returned to the first neuron for use in carrying the next message. Dopamine transporter chemicals, called DAT, carry the dopamine out of the synapse and back to the first neuron. In a SPECT scan, a chemical "tag" called I-ioflupane (DaTscan) is injected into the bloodstream and attaches itself to the DAT. A camera called a gamma camera can detect the concentration of the tag in the brain, and therefore can detect the concentration of the DAT. In diseases such as PD and Lewy body dementia, this signal is decreased. In this way the function of dopamine-producing neurons can be evaluated.

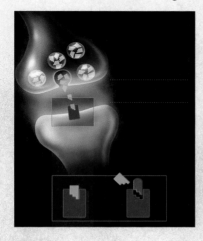

Neurotransmitters such as dopamine "dock" in the receptors of receiving neurons.

parkinsonism is sorting out all the possible causes for the symptoms. It is estimated that as many as 25 percent of people with PD are diagnosed with something other than PD and that as many as 40 percent are never diagnosed at all. The early symptoms may come and go, or the person may ignore them for years, until they get too debilitating. The four hallmark symptoms may not all appear in every patient. For example, approximately 25 to 30 percent of PD patients do not have early tremors. A diagnosis of PD may be missed in younger people because of their age, or an older person with a stooped-over posture may be diagnosed with osteoporosis (bone thinning). "Parkinson's is a different disease for every person," says Patsy Dalton. "It's extremely individual. You can't say any one person is going to progress in a certain way. We know people who have had Parkinson's for 30 years and they're still playing golf, and we know people who have Parkinson's for two years and they're gone now."[17]

A doctor checks a patient for Parkinson's. As many as 25 percent of people with PD are diagnosed with something other than PD, and as many as 40 percent are never diagnosed at all.

Getting an accurate diagnosis of PD is further complicated because there are no simple blood tests or X-rays that can pinpoint the disease. Electroencephalograms can record some of the brain's electrical activity, but they are not helpful for diagnosing PD. Blood tests, other lab tests, and other kinds of diagnostic tests can be used to rule out other possible causes for some of the symptoms, such as thyroid disease or vascular disease, but this ruling out process can take weeks or months. The wait to find out what is wrong can be frustrating for the patient and his or her family.

History and Physical Examination

Eventually, the symptoms of PD become persistent enough for the person to see a doctor. The first thing the doctor will do when a patient arrives at the office is take a thorough account of the patient's medical history. The doctor will talk with the patient and the family to learn about the general nature of the patient's symptoms—what symptoms the patient has been having, how long he or she has been having them, how severe they are, and at what times they are better or worse. The doctor will review the patient's medical history to see whether there are any other health issues present that may be causing the symptoms. The doctor will ask about family history, specifically whether there are family members who have had similar symptoms. The doctor will also ask about the patient's daily activities, such as work (if the patient is employed), what medications he or she is on, and what chemicals he or she may be exposed to.

Along with a thorough medical history, the doctor will do a complete physical examination of the patient. He or she will assess the patient's heart and lungs and order blood tests that indicate liver function, thyroid function, and other general health indicators. These tests can also help rule out other possible causes for the symptoms.

Neurological Examination

Following the initial history and physical exam, if the doctor suspects that PD or some other neurological disorder is causing the symptoms, the patient may be referred to a neurologist—a physician who specializes in disorders of the brain and nervous system. This physician will do additional evaluations more specifically related to the neurological symptoms the patient is having. The evaluation will start with an interview that focuses on the patient's neurological function. The doctor will ask questions related to things such as difficulty with small hand movements (writing, buttoning shirts, handling utensils, and so on), difficulty with larger movements (starting to walk or getting up from chairs, out of cars, or out of bed), eating and swallowing, muscle stiffness, sleep problems, voice changes, keeping balance or falling or fainting, and other questions that assess neurological functioning.

After this information is collected, a physical examination that also looks closely at neurological functioning will be done. This kind of exam will look at the patient's movements, reflexes, posture, gait, balance, coordination, and strength. The doctor may have the patient perform tasks such as sitting down and getting up, walking down the hallway, turning around, or lifting various weights. The doctor will observe for slowness of movement, freezing, arm swing, resting tremors, or other repetitive hand and finger motions such as finger tapping or "pill rolling." The doctor will also assess speech quality, facial expression, and sensory functions such as vision, skin sensation, and smell.

Imaging Studies
Regular X-rays of the brain are not helpful in diagnosing PD because the cause of the disease takes place on a microscopic level and is not visible on an X-ray. There are, however, several kinds of advanced imaging tests that can help rule out other causes for the patient's symptoms. A computed tomography (CT) scan combines X-rays with computers to provide a detailed image of the internal structure of the brain. CT scans are good for finding tumors, swelling, or other structural abnormalities that may be causing the problem. A magnetic resonance image (MRI) provides very clear images of the inside of the brain without using X-rays. Instead, an MRI uses

The Story of MPTP

In 1976 a twenty-three-year-old chemistry student named Barry Kidston decided to use his chemistry skills to manufacture an illegal drug called MPPP, an artificial form of heroin. One of the by-products of MPPP production is a highly toxic chemical that is abbreviated MPTP. Unknown to Kidston, his batch of MPPP was contaminated with MPTP. Within three days of using his concoction, he began showing Parkinson's-like symptoms. Eventually, he became completely immobilized. He was treated with levodopa, and his symptoms improved somewhat, but eighteen months later he died of a cocaine overdose. An examination of his brain showed extensive destruction of the dopaminergic neurons in the substantia nigra of his brain.

Six years later, a group of six people were diagnosed with severe parkinsonism after also using MPPP contaminated with MPTP. Unlike typical parkinsonism, their symptoms progressed over weeks rather than months or years. These people had become frozen and could barely speak or walk, and they could no longer care for themselves. Their neurologist, J. William Langston, wrote about their story in his 2014 book *The Case of the Frozen Addicts.* These cases triggered a new approach to Parkinson's disease research, using MPTP to induce PD symptoms in test animals. Unlike other drugs that can cause parkinsonism by interfering with dopamine production, MPTP caused its symptoms by actually destroying the neurons themselves. Out of this unfortunate incident came new knowledge about nerve cell death in PD and new drugs to treat it. It also focused attention on the potential for environmental toxins to cause parkinsonism.

radio waves, a computer, and a large magnetic device to make the images.

CTs and MRIs provide detailed pictures of the structure of the brain, but in PD patients, these tests often look normal. Another imaging study, called a positron emission tomography

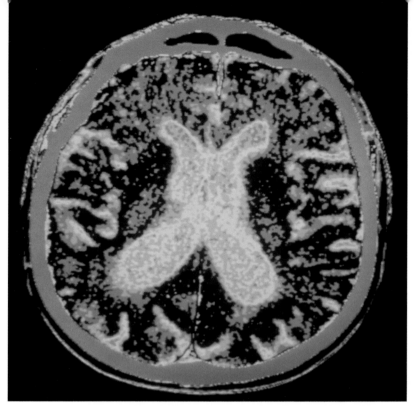

A CT scan of a PD patient's brain. Parkinson's has caused the ventricles (in blue) to increase in size as brain tissue loses density with the death of cells.

(PET) scan, uses a special kind of camera and a radioactive chemical called a tracer to study the actual functioning of the cells of the brain. A PET scan can provide information about the brain's blood flow and cell activity and can help identify disorders such as cancers, Alzheimer's disease, epilepsy, strokes, and certain mental illnesses. If PD is suspected, the tracer chemical used is one specifically designed to study cell function in the areas of the brain that control movement. The tracer emits tiny charged particles called positrons. The special camera records the location and density of the positrons in the cells and turns the recording into a picture that gives an indication of the function of the cells.

A Waiting Game

Unfortunately for patients who are hoping for a diagnosis, all these tests are more helpful for determining what the problem is not, rather than what it is. In the absence of a definitive test that can specifically diagnose PD, there may be nothing left to do except wait and see how the symptoms change over time. William J. Weiner explains:

> Sometimes, all the doctor can do is wait for several months, then reexamine the patient to determine whether the changes in the symptoms are typical of true Parkinson's. Delay in diagnosis can be frustrating for both patients and physicians. But Parkinson's is a serious disease, and the diagnosis must be accurate so the doctor can choose appropriate therapies and people can have an idea of how their disease will change in the future.[18]

As weeks and months pass, additional symptoms may appear, such as problems with memory, changes in personality, depression, anxiety, problems with eye movements, or problems with bladder or bowel control. These kinds of signs often point to other neurological disorders such as Alzheimer's disease, Lewy body dementia, PSP, or MSA, and they may help zero in on an accurate diagnosis.

Most of the other causes of parkinsonism do not respond well to drugs used to treat PD, especially the drug levodopa. This fact makes levodopa useful for diagnosing PD as well as for treating it. If, after testing and observation, PD appears to be the most likely diagnosis, a levodopa "challenge" may be done. If the person's symptoms respond dramatically to levodopa, then PD is more likely the problem. If the person does not improve, or if improvement is only temporary, it becomes more likely that his or her parkinsonism is caused by something other than PD. The levodopa challenge is not 100 percent accurate in all cases, but it can be helpful in some patients.

After extensive testing and observation, and after other causes of parkinsonism have been ruled out, the doctor may confirm the diagnosis of PD. At this point, treatment decisions can be made and treatment can begin.

CHAPTER FOUR

Treating Parkinson's Disease

James Parkinson was the first to accurately describe the characteristic signs of the affliction that he called paralysis agitans and how they progress over time. By doing this, he established PD as a discrete disorder, separate from other illnesses with similar symptoms. Soon after, other neurologists began to add their own observations. The most valuable additions came from a French neurologist named Jean-Martin Charcot (1825–1893). Charcot further defined the motor symptoms of PD by distinguishing muscle rigidity, weakness, and bradykinesia as separate symptoms. He is also credited with making sure that the disease was given the name Parkinson's disease to honor the man (too humble to name it after himself) who first described it. Charcot also introduced the first effective treatment for PD, and as is so often the case in science and medicine, it happened by pure chance.

At the time, in the late 1860s, a drug called hyoscyamine (hye-oh-SI-a-meen) was being used to control drooling in patients with neurological diseases. When Charcot gave hyoscyamine to PD patients, he noticed almost right away that the drug brought a dramatic improvement in their tremors and muscle rigidity. For the next one hundred years, hyoscyamine and drugs like it were the main treatment method for PD.

Levodopa

A breakthrough in PD treatment came in 1957 when the function of dopamine as a neurotransmitter was discovered by Swedish scientists Arvid Carlsson and Nils-Åke Hillarp. Four years later, Austrian biochemist Oleh Hornykiewicz established dopamine deficiency as the cause of PD. Unfortunately, dopamine itself cannot be given as a medication for PD because it is unable to cross the barrier between the blood vessels and the brain—the so-called blood-brain barrier. However, a chemical called levodopa (also called L-dopa) can easily cross the barrier, and once it gets into the brain, it is converted into dopamine. Levodopa is naturally made in the bodies of humans, some animals, and even some plants. It is called a precursor because it can be converted into several other neurotransmitters as well as dopamine.

When levodopa was first introduced as a treatment for PD in 1969, the results were dramatic, especially in patients with severe symptoms. "Shortly after starting a course of treatment," says Canadian neurologist Donald Calne, "one of my patients complained of severe hip pain. . . . Before L-Dopa, the patient had been bedridden; [the arthritis in his hip] had been 'silent.' After starting the treatment, he regained the use of his legs and the arthritis proclaimed its presence."[19]

Levodopa offered many patients hope for significant improvement in their symptoms and still does today, but it cannot cure Parkinson's disease. Today there is still no cure for the illness, but there are ways to treat it and its symptoms. The goals of treatment for PD depend on the particular symptoms the patient is having and how his or her life is being affected by them. Treatment decisions are customized for each individual patient, depending on his or her specific needs. In most cases goals of treatment include maintaining quality of life as much as possible; maximizing independence; improving mobility and body function; reducing tremors and muscle stiffness; improving balance, posture, and walking; decreasing depression and anxiety; and maintaining mental sharpness. Caring for the PD patient is truly a team effort.

The Treatment Team

Many different kinds of health professionals take part in the treatment decisions for each patient, depending on the patient's particular needs. The team members work closely together to coordinate their services so that the patient receives the maximum benefit from treatment. They also remain in frequent contact with the patient and his or her family to make sure treatment is having its desired effects and that the patient is progressing.

Jean-Martin Charcot

Jean-Martin Charcot (shar-KO) is often called the "father of neurology." His name is associated with more than a dozen medical conditions, including Charcot disease. This is better known as amyotrophic lateral sclerosis (ALS), or Lou Gehrig's disease. His work revolutionized the fields of both neuroscience and psychology.

Charcot was born on November 29, 1825, in Paris, France. He completed medical school at age twenty-three and went to work at the Hospital de la Salpêtrière in Paris. He distinguished himself right away with his work and became a professor of pathological anatomy at the University of Paris in 1872. He became renowned for his teaching style, using real patients to demonstrate symptoms and employing the new technology of photography to illustrate his lectures. Charcot attracted students from all over Europe. Some of his more famous students included Austrian neurologist Sigmund Freud, French neurologist Joseph Babinski, and French physician Georges Gilles de la Tourette, for whom Tourette syndrome is named. Over the thirty-three years he spent at the Salpêtrière Hospital, his work brought international fame to the institution as one of the best in the world for neurological and psychiatric disorders.

Charcot described the pattern of blood circulation in the brain and studied the functions of several parts of the brain. He is well known for his work on hypnosis as a treatment for "hysteria," an

The leader of the treatment team is the neurologist. A neurologist is a physician with special training in diagnosing and treating diseases and disorders of the brain, spine, nervous system, and muscles. He or she may also have special training in movement disorders such as PD. The neurologist is in charge of the medical management of the patient and decides what other services the patient needs. He or she will do the initial evaluation of the patient, order the necessary testing

early term for mental illness. He was the first to describe ALS and multiple sclerosis (MS) as unique diseases separate from other nerve disorders and was able to distinguish the tremors of Parkinson's disease from those of MS. The three major signs of MS are referred to as Charcot's triad. His detailed descriptions (along with those of two other scientists) of a muscle-wasting nerve disorder led to the disease being named Charcot-Marie-Tooth disease. His work on the

illness that James Parkinson called paralysis agitans led to a new understanding of the disease, which he renamed Parkinson's disease. Charcot died in France in 1893. His son Jean-Baptiste, an accomplished explorer, named Charcot Island in Antarctica in honor of his father.

French neurologist Jean-Martin Charcot (1825–1893) further defined the motor symptoms of PD by distinguishing muscle rigidity, weakness, and bradykinesia as separate symptoms.

and medications, monitor the patient's response to treatment, and coordinate the services of the other members of the team.

Rehabilitation specialists include physical therapists, occupational therapists, and speech therapists. Physical therapists work with PD patients to improve mobility, balance, strength, endurance, and flexibility. They help PD patients improve their ability to stand up, walk, and maintain good posture. Occupational therapists help people with injuries or disabilities improve their ability to perform independently the tasks of everyday living and working. These activities of daily living include simple tasks such as writing, bathing, dressing, and eating, as well as more complex tasks such as cooking, traveling, and shopping. Occupational therapists can also help patients with safety issues in the home. Speech and language therapists help people overcome difficulties with speaking and swallowing. For PD patients, such problems include low speaking

Treatment teams for Parkinson's typically include physical therapists, occupational therapists, and speech therapists under the direction of a neurologist. Pictured here is a team using an MRI to check a PD patient's response to therapy.

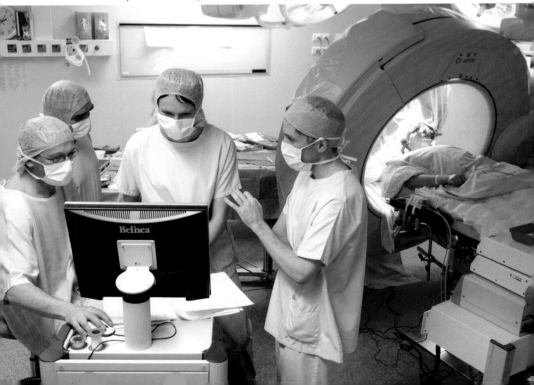

Treating PD Before Levodopa

One of the earliest medications for treating PD was hyoscyamine; the benefit of hyoscyamine for PD patients was one of Jean-Martin Charcot's most important discoveries. Hyoscyamine is in a class of drugs called anticholinergics, which decrease secretions in several organs and relax smooth muscle spasms. Anticholinergics were introduced in the late 1800s. They were originally made from an herb called *Atropa belladonna,* and at that time they were called belladonna alkaloids.

Belladonna, also called "deadly nightshade," can be somewhat hazardous because it can cause dizziness, excessive drowsiness, and hallucinations. It was used as a poison during the time of the Roman Empire. Despite its dangers, it was used in the Middle Ages as an anesthetic for surgery. It was also commonly used in the 1800s by wealthy women in Europe to make their pupils dilate. It was thought that large pupils made the eyes more attractive, and that is how it came to be called "belladonna," Italian for "beautiful woman." Hyoscyamine and other anticholinergics such as scopolamine and atropine are used today for treating a variety of bladder, stomach, and intestinal problems, as well as the excessive salivation for which Charcot prescribed it. They are not used in the later stages of PD, because they counteract drugs that increase alertness and attention.

volume, slurred speech, or stuttering. Speech and language therapists conduct swallowing studies and help patients improve their ability to swallow so that they can get the nutrition they need and avoid choking.

Many PD patients, particularly younger patients, may experience a certain amount of emotional difficulty dealing with the diagnosis of a life-changing, incurable disease such as PD. Depression and anxiety related to PD are common, especially in younger patients and in older patients in the later stages.

For these patients the services of a trained mental health provider such as a family therapist, psychologist, psychiatrist, or counselor can help them and their family cope with the diagnosis and help them view their future in terms of the positive rather than the negative. Individual as well as family therapy are available, depending on the particular needs of the patient and family.

Eating properly is extremely helpful for PD patients. A well-balanced diet helps maintain strength, alertness, and energy levels. Getting the proper nutrition can be a challenge for patients who have difficulty eating or swallowing. They may have little appetite because of depression or the side effects of their medications. They may simply forget to eat regularly. A registered dietician can help PD patients and their families make sure patients are getting the proper nutrients every day by identifying favorite foods, providing nutrients and calories in a form that is easier for patients to chew and swallow, and by providing easily prepared and nutrient-dense options such as protein shakes.

Drugs for Parkinson's Disease

Since the introduction of hyoscyamine in the 1860s and levodopa in the 1960s, many newer medications have been developed and are available to treat PD symptoms. As more is learned about these new drugs, as well as the older ones, they can be put to their best use so that the patient's quality of life is improved as much as possible. The two major goals of drug treatment for PD are to increase the levels of available dopamine in the brain and to minimize the symptoms.

Levodopa remains the drug of choice for treating the symptoms of PD, especially slow movement and muscle rigidity, but it does have many side effects. The problem is that levodopa is also converted into dopamine in the peripheral nervous system—the part of the nervous system that is outside the brain and spinal cord. When levodopa is given as a drug, it can result in too much dopamine in the body, which causes many of the side effects. Some of the more common side ef-

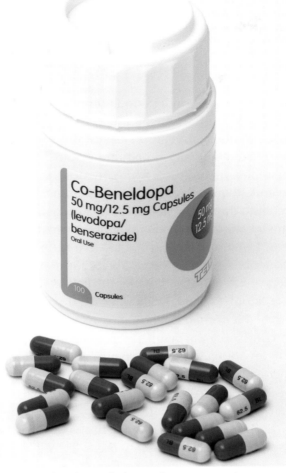

Levodopa remains the drug of choice for treating the symptoms of PD, especially slow movement and muscle rigidity, but it does have many side effects.

fects include allergic reactions, dizziness, low blood pressure, nausea, hair loss, irregular heartbeat, confusion, vivid dreams, hallucinations, and extreme emotional behaviors.

One way to counteract the side effects caused by too much dopamine is to give levodopa in combination with another drug that inhibits, or suppresses, its conversion to dopamine in the peripheral nervous system. Carbidopa is an example of this type of drug and is often given in combination with levodopa. The most commonly used levodopa-carbidopa combination drug is called Sinemet. Sinemet has few short-term side effects, but it has additional side effects when used for a long time, including involuntary muscle movements (dyskinesias), restlessness, and confusion.

If, after a long time on levodopa or a combination drug, the drug is no longer effective or the side effects are becoming too severe, an alternative is a class of drugs called dopamine agonists. There are many dopamine agonists available today; some examples include Neupro (rotigotine), Mirapex (pramipexole), and Requip (ropinirole). Dopamine agonists are not converted into dopamine like levodopa is; instead, they act like dopamine by stimulating cells that are normally stimulated by dopamine. Dopamine agonists can be used alone or together with levodopa. They may be used early in PD treatment in order to delay having to use levodopa. One especially fast-acting dopamine agonist, apomorphine, is used in cases of freezing such as when a person cannot start to walk or cannot get up from a chair. Dopamine agonists have fewer long-term side effects than levodopa, but they have a higher risk of short-term side effects, many of which are similar to those for levodopa.

Two other kinds of drugs work by blocking the action of chemicals in the body that break down levodopa. This helps increase the amount of levodopa that gets into the brain so that it can be converted into dopamine. They are called COMT inhibitors and MAO-B inhibitors. Examples are Comtan (entacapone), Tasmar (tolcapone), and Eldepryl (selegilene). These drugs are given along with levodopa because they do not help PD symptoms by themselves. Because these drugs can increase the amount of levodopa in the brain, they are useful during wearing-off periods between doses of levodopa. They are also helpful for patients who want better relief for their symptoms but do not want to increase their dose of levodopa. Patients who want to take only one pill can take a combination pill that contains levodopa, carbidopa, and one of these inhibitor drugs.

Surgery for Parkinson's Disease

Surgical interventions for PD began in the 1930s and were mainly done to reduce tremors. The procedures were very risky and had severe complications such as paralysis. Results were unpredictable and unreliable. By the 1950s neurologists and neurosurgeons had a better understanding of how different parts of the brain responded to surgery. The risks went down and the results improved. During the 1950s and 1960s, before levodopa was developed, two surgical procedures for PD were done that target specific parts of the brain thought to be involved with PD—the globus pallidus (or simply "globus") and the thalamus.

Neurology

Neurology (from the Greek words *neuron* and *logia,* or "study of nerves") is a medical specialty related to disorders of the nervous system, including the brain, spinal cord, nerves, and muscles. A neurologist is a physician specially trained to take care of patients with these kinds of disorders. Neurologists may also take part in any or all phases of the research process. To become a neurologist, one must graduate from college and then from medical school. After medical school comes three to four years of specialized training, called a residency, in neurology. Some neurologists complete even more specialized training, called a fellowship, in a particular area of neurology such as stroke care, head trauma, neuromuscular diseases like MS or ALS, or movement disorders like PD.

A surgeon who specializes in surgery on the nervous system is called a neurosurgeon. After medical school, future neurosurgeons complete seven years of residency in surgery and neurosurgery. They may then do a fellowship in a more specialized area such as pediatric (child) neurosurgery, head and spinal trauma, or neurological cancer surgery.

The globus pallidus, like the substantia nigra, is part of the basal ganglia, which regulates subconscious muscle movements. The globus acts somewhat like the brakes in a car. It inhibits, or slows down, the effects of other areas in the brain that excite, or stimulate, the muscles. The inhibitory and excitatory areas in the brain work together to allow people to move smoothly. If there is an imbalance, movement problems result. In PD the globus is overactive, which causes movement to slow down. A surgical procedure called pallidotomy destroys the globus so that it cannot have this effect. Pallidotomy can significantly lessen the muscle rigidity, tremors, balance problems, and bradykinesia of PD when medication is no longer effective.

A CT scan shows the path of a surgical probe used to treat PD. The procedure is known as pallidotomy.

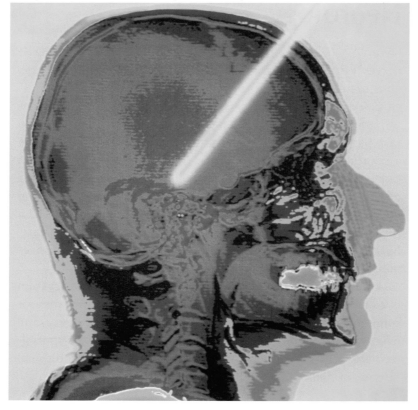

During a pallidotomy, the patient is awake but sedated with medications. A small area of the scalp is numbed with an anesthetic medication injected into the skin, and a small opening is made in the skull. Using sophisticated guiding technology such as MRI, the globus pallidus is located, and a tiny probe is inserted into it. The probe is then chilled to an extremely cold temperature. The cold destroys the globus so that it can no longer function to slow muscle movement.

Thalamotomy is similar to pallidotomy and is done in a similar way, except that it targets a different structure called the thalamus. Located very near the globus, the thalamus processes and relays brain activity sent from other areas, including the globus. Thalamotomy destroys the thalamus so that it cannot relay abnormal brain activity. This procedure is rarely done today. It is done mainly for treating very severe, one-sided tremors that have not responded to medication. It does not work well for bradykinesia or balance problems. Both procedures declined in use when levodopa was introduced in the late 1960s.

Deep Brain Stimulation

Pallidotomy and thalamotomy further declined with the development of a newer procedure called deep brain stimulation (DBS). DBS is similar to pallidotomy and thalamotomy in that it is used to block abnormal activity, but without actually destroying any brain tissue.

In DBS tiny electrodes are placed into the target areas of the brain, most commonly the globus or the thalamus. The other end of the electrodes are connected to a small device called an impulse generator, which is implanted under the skin on the upper chest. The impulse generator sends constant electrical impulses into the target areas and interferes with their function without destroying them. The generator can be programmed with a computer, and the patient can turn it on or off. DBS has been shown to improve PD symptoms such as tremor, bradykinesia, and balance and speech problems, although some benefits last longer than others. "There are certain things it will treat dramatically, like the tremors," says Michael Rezac, a movement disorders specialist. "It will also help slowness and stiffness, and we're able to reduce medications significantly."[20]

Gamma Knife Radiation

Some patients whose medications are no longer effective cannot, for various reasons, have a surgical procedure for their symptoms. Patients on anticoagulant (blood-thinning) medications, for example, are at too high a risk for bleeding during or after surgery. For these and other patients, an alternative therapy is Gamma Knife radiation. A Gamma Knife is not really a knife at all, but a form of radiation therapy that uses gamma rays to treat various kinds of brain abnormalities.

During a Gamma Knife procedure, a special frame is fitted onto the patient's head that helps hold the head steady and helps aim the gamma rays at the target location in the brain. The patient lies on a bed that slides into the Gamma Knife machine. The Gamma Knife machine emits about two hundred gamma rays at the desired target. The rays come to a focus point in the target area and do not damage the surrounding brain tissue on their way there. Gamma Knife radiation does not require an incision in the skin or a hole in the skull, and the patient cannot feel the radiation. During the treatment, which can take several hours depending on the size of the target area, the patient and the doctors communicate with each other using a microphone.

Treating Nonmotor PD Symptoms

Surgical procedures can be highly effective for treating the motor symptoms of PD such as tremors, bradykinesia, and balance or gait problems. Common nonmotor problems of PD, however, such as cognitive issues, sleep issues, speech problems, and mood disorders, also need attention and treatment if they become significant enough to interfere with daily life.

Cognitive issues such as problems with attention, thinking, and memory can have a significant impact on a person's abil-

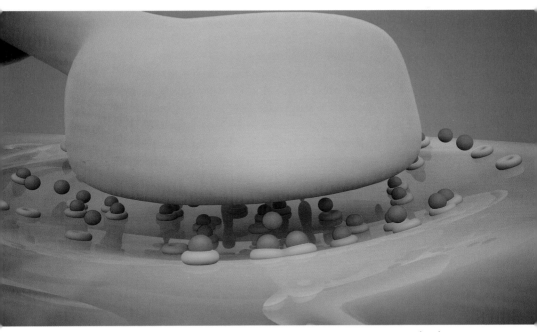

Acetylcholine is the most common neurotransmitter in the brain. PD medications work to increase the amount of acetylcholine in the brain.

ity to carry out activities of daily living. For cognitive issues, treatment generally involves a combination of medication and behavioral modifications. The main class of medications for cognitive problems is called acetylcholinesterase inhibitors. Although these medications do not actually improve cognitive problems, they can help slow their progression and keep them from getting worse. They work by increasing the amount of a neurotransmitter in the brain called acetylcholine (abbreviated ACh). ACh is the most common neurotransmitter in the brain. ACh is involved in learning, memory, and maintaining attention and alertness. Outside the brain, ACh works to activate and regulate muscle movement.

Cognitive problems can also be treated by teaching the patient to use the cognitive abilities they still have to help compensate for problem areas. For example, a person with memory difficulties might be taught to organize daily activities

in a more regular and structured way to make it easier to remember to do them. A person with attention or focus problems
can be helped by simplifying the home environment to reduce
distractions.

About 90 percent of PD patients experience a variety of
sleep-related problems such as insomnia, daytime sleepiness, vivid dreams or nightmares, or sleep apnea (periods of
not breathing during sleep). Sleep problems can be caused
by depression or anxiety, muscle cramps, or side effects of
medications. Sleep problems can become cyclic. For example,
sleep apnea or nightmares can cause insomnia at night, which
causes daytime sleepiness, which worsens insomnia at night.
Sleep problems may be treated with an extra dose of PD medication at night or an over-the-counter sleep aid. Sleep apnea
can be remedied with the use of a device called a CPAP (con-
tinuous positive airway pressure) machine, which helps keep
airways open and improves the quality of sleep.

Speech problems such as voice volume and strength are
treated by a speech pathologist. A widely used therapy for
PD patients is called the Lee Silverman Voice Treatment. This
therapy is a structured set of exercises, done four days a week
for four weeks, that are designed to strengthen volume, pitch,
and voice quality. Another strategy for voice problems involves
injections of a protein called collagen into vocal cords that do
not close all the way during speech. Incomplete closure of the
vocal cords can cause weakness in the strength of the voice.

The most common mood disorders of PD are depression
and anxiety. Both of these disorders are treated with a combination of medication and psychological counseling. Most patients with depression and/or anxiety are treated with a class
of drugs called selective serotonin reuptake inhibitors (SSRIs).
Examples of SSRI's include fluoxetine (Prozac), sertraline
(Zoloft) and paroxetine (Paxil). SSRIs work by increasing the
amount of a neurotransmitter called serotonin in the brain. Serotonin has many functions in the brain, one of which is regulating mood. There are other non-SSRI medications that work
for depression by increasing levels of other neurotransmitters

in the brain, such as dopamine and norepinephrine. Anxiety is also treated with an older class of drugs called benzodiazepines. These drugs target another brain chemical called GABA. Some common benzodiazepines include diazepam (Valium), clonazepam (Klonopin), and alprazolam (Xanax).

Medications for depression and anxiety are commonly used in combination with psychological counseling or psychotherapy. Counseling is conducted by a licensed counselor or social worker, psychologist, psychiatrist, or specially trained psychiatric nurse. It can be done one-on-one with the therapist, in a group setting, or as a family. Counseling provides emotional support and education for the patient and family. A very effective approach is called cognitive behavioral therapy, which teaches patients and families to get rid of negative thinking and behavior patterns and look at the challenges they face with a more positive and constructive attitude.

Complementary Treatments for PD

Complementary treatments are treatments that have not been scientifically proved to be safe or effective for a particular condition. They are not meant to be used in place of traditional medical therapies but can be used along with traditional therapies. This is especially true for PD. "There is pretty much no getting around that Parkinson's disease patients will need traditional medication eventually," says Melanie Brandabur, clinical director of the Parkinson's Institute and Clinical Center in Sunnyvale, California. "A lot of people start off with the idea that they want to avoid pharmaceuticals, but that isn't possible in the long term."[21]

Although complementary treatments cannot replace medical treatment, they can often help relieve symptoms for many patients. For example, massage therapy can help relieve muscle rigidity and soreness. Some patients report that acupuncture, an ancient Chinese treatment that is used for many purposes, helps them with tremors and muscle stiffness. Other traditional Asian practices such as yoga, tai chi, and meditation promote relaxation, help relieve stress and anxiety, and

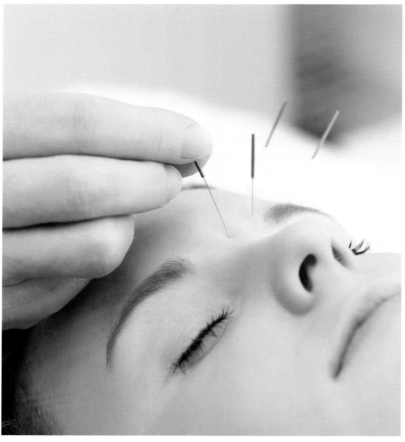

Some PD patients report that acupuncture, an ancient Chinese treatment that is used for many purposes, helps them with tremors and muscle stiffness.

provide beneficial slow-movement exercise for stiff or painful muscles. Dietary supplements called nutraceuticals, such as coenzyme Q10 and creatine, help support energy levels and muscle function. Vitamin B_{12} is important for brain and spinal cord health.

CHAPTER FIVE

Living with Parkinson's Disease

When Lizbeth Muller's father was diagnosed with PD, it came as somewhat of a surprise to the whole family. Lizbeth, however, had had a feeling for some time that something was wrong. She says:

> To be honest even prior to his diagnosis, I had a feeling he might have Parkinson's. He had a lot of shaking in his hands which I found out of the ordinary. He kept saying it was his nerves. I think he was in denial at first because he didn't know much about the disease and how important it is to catch it in its early stages. Then my dad went to his primary care physician. As soon as he saw my dad shuffling his feet, he said, "I think your father is suffering from Parkinson's." He sent my father to a neurologist, who confirmed the diagnosis.[22]

Few diseases change the direction of a person's life as profoundly as Parkinson's disease. PD affects almost every aspect of daily life, from simple tasks such as buttoning a shirt to more complex activities such as traveling or planning for retirement. For many, the diagnosis comes as a complete surprise. This is especially true for younger patients. For others, such as Lizbeth Muller, the diagnosis simply confirms what they and their families have suspected for a long time but did not know for sure. Some patients have a strong network of support from family, friends, or other sources. Others may feel very alone and frightened. The good news is that there are many ways for the PD patient and his or her family to continue to live life to the fullest.

PD is, by its very nature, a very difficult disease to understand. Just as the array of symptoms experienced and the nature of their progression is unique to each patient, so are the adaptations that must be made to accommodate them. One of the first steps to take is to become as fully educated as possible about the disease. Knowledge is a powerful weapon when fighting a disease like PD. Talking with health professionals, reading books, articles, and reliable Internet sources, and interacting with others who are also dealing with PD are all good ways to get ready for what lies ahead. Having a good idea of what to expect allows patients and families to anticipate future needs with as few surprises as possible and to make necessary preparations ahead of time. In this way living with PD is made as stress free as possible.

Adapting Activities of Daily Living

Activities of daily living are common, everyday activities such as bathing, dressing, cooking, and cleaning. Many patients in the early stages of PD are able to live independently in their own homes, and at first there may not be many adaptations that need to be made. Occasional checks by a neighbor or a visiting nurse or home health aide may be all that is necessary to make sure the patients' needs are being met, that their environment is safe, and that they are taking their medications properly. As the disease progresses, however, ways of carrying out one's activities of daily living may have to be modified in order to maintain independence, safety, and quality of life. Most adaptations become necessary because of tremors, loss of hand dexterity, and problems with walking and balance.

Basic hygiene can be a challenge. Showering can be done sitting down, using a shower chair and handrails installed in the

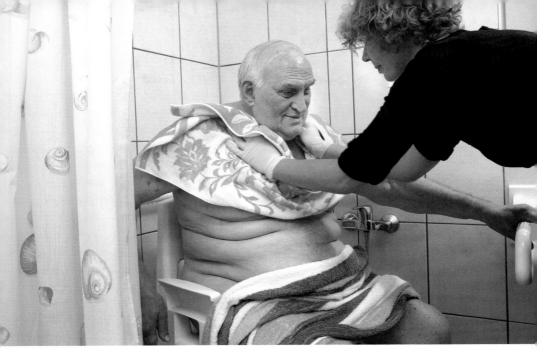

For Parkinson's patients basic hygiene can be a challenge. Showering can be done sitting down, using a shower chair, and handrails installed in the shower provide extra stability and safety.

shower to provide extra stability and safety. Specially designed walk-in tubs have a door in the side that allows a person to just walk into the tub, rather than step over the side. They also have seats built in so that the person can bathe sitting down. A handheld shower hose helps distribute water, and sponges or cloths with a handle to hold on to and a pouch to hold the soap help prevent dropping the soap. Liquid bath soap in a pump bottle is even easier. Nonskid bathmats on the bottom of the shower or tub and rubber-backed floor mats on the bathroom floor help eliminate slips and falls. Grooming also can be done sitting down, for comfort and safety. Toothbrushes, combs, and hairbrushes with large handles are easier for patients to hold. Electric razors and electric toothbrushes are safer and easier to use than regular ones.

The normally simple act of getting dressed each day can present a major hurdle for the PD patient. Loss of balance makes it difficult to put on pants or shoes. Tremors and loss of hand coordination interferes with buttoning shirts or tying shoes. Frozen shoulder or other muscle stiffness can make it hard to put on a coat or sweater. Getting dressed while sitting can help maintain balance and prevent falls. If hand tremors are a problem, clothing with elastic, larger buttons, zippers, or Velcro flaps can be easier to use. Slip-on shoes or shoes with elastic laces or Velcro flaps are easier to put on than lace-up shoes. Devices such as dressing sticks, sock donners, and long-handled shoehorns assist with putting on coats, socks, and shoes.

Safety in the Home

Problems with balance, coordination, and gait can present a significant safety hazard to those with PD. Getting up from a chair or a bed, turning around, or having to react quickly can easily lead to falls. Freezing can cause falls because episodes are unpredictable and because well-meaning attempts by others to make the person start moving can cause them to lose their balance. There are many ways that PD patients can make their home a safer place so that they can maintain their independence as long as possible.

In the bathroom, assistive devices such as shower chairs or seats, grab bars, nonskid floor mats, elevated toilet seats, and walk-in tubs all create a safer environment. Safety measures for the bedroom can include a bed (with side rails, if necessary) that is easy to get in and out of and is not too high or too low. A nightlight or flashlight by the bed helps if it is necessary to get up during the night. Overhead room lights can be fitted with a remote control so that they can be turned on and off from the bed. A phone next to the bed is important in case the person needs to call for help at night. Socks with nonskid soles help prevent slipping.

The kitchen is one of the more hazardous areas in the home. Working smoke alarms are important in any home and need regular battery changes. Tremors can make it more likely that items may be dropped, so sturdy plastic plates, bowls, and glasses prevent the hazard of broken glass. Utensils with built-up handles are easier to hold on to and control. Using sharp utensils such as knives can be difficult; the person with

The Liftware Spoon

For people with disorders that cause hand tremors, such as essential tremor or PD, a major challenge can be eating foods such as soups that require a spoon. The tremor causes the food to spill or fall off the spoon, which can be frustrating and embarrassing for the person and can interfere with getting the nutrition he or she needs.

A new kind of spoon, called the Liftware spoon, helps with this problem. The Liftware spoon contains a battery, a microchip, and a motion detector in the handle that detect the direction and force of a person's tremors and then move the spoon in the opposite direction to balance out the motion of the tremor. This helps keep the bowl of the spoon stabilized so that food stays on it better. The spoon can cancel out as much as 70 percent of the effect of the tremor. The spoon can be detached from the handle for washing, and the handle can be set into a dock to recharge the battery.

The idea for the Liftware spoon was inspired by tremor cancellation technology that was developed to help soldiers hold their rifles steady. It is also similar to motion cancellation features in cameras and cell phones. The company that makes Liftware plans to develop other attachments for the handle, such as a fork and a key holder.

tremors may need help with meal preparation or may choose to use frozen or boxed prepared foods. Assistive devices such as long-handled reachers are helpful for reaching items on upper shelves or in lower cabinets.

Simply getting around the house safely can be a major challenge. Throughout the house, adequate lighting is very important for safety. If there are area rugs on the floor, they should lie flat, with no curled-up edges, and they should be firmly attached to the floor. Wires and cords should be out of the way. Stairs should have nonskid surfaces attached, and a sturdy banister is essential. If necessary, an automated stair-lift device can be installed so that the person can get upstairs while seated. Emergency phone numbers should be kept available near the telephone. The use of a medical alert device can be very valuable for summoning help in an emergency. Assistive devices such as canes or walkers may be needed for extra stability. Jeanne and Dan Crace had to retire from their business when Jeanne's mobility became an issue of safety. "Later on," she says, "mobility became a serious problem, my shuffling got worse and the freeze-ups became ever present, I was falling frequently, and was lucky I only had broken ribs on a couple of occasions. It became necessary to use a scooter, walker, and a cane. Dan has always been there to help me and encourage me when tasks became difficult."[23]

Driving with PD

Driving represents another important safety issue for the person living with PD. Being able to drive one's own car is a major indicator of independence, self-reliance, and control in a person's life. Driving lets people get where they need to go, when they need to go there—to work or social events, the doctor's office, the grocery store, or another person's home. People with PD may be unwilling to give up their ability to drive whenever they need or want to, but PD can affect a person's ability to drive safely. Muscle stiffness or tremors in the arms, hands, or legs can make it difficult to turn the steering wheel or depress the gas or brake pedal. Slowness of movement decreases a person's ability to react quickly to road conditions or other drivers. The stooped posture of PD can make it harder for the person to see the road and surrounding areas. Some PD patients experience a condition called blepharospasm (*blepharo* means "eyelid"), in which their eyes close involuntarily. Cognitive impairments can cause problems with paying attention to the road, making decisions, or remembering how to get from one place to another. In addition, some PD medications can cause side effects such as confusion, memory problems, drowsiness, or blurred vision. Driving is a potentially hazardous activity that requires full concentration, attention, and the ability to react quickly. All these things can be impaired in PD.

In the early stages of PD, most people can still drive safely, especially if their medications are effectively controlling their symptoms. Certain extra precautions may be necessary, however. For example, driving at night or during rush hour may need to be avoided when possible. As PD progresses, there may come a time when driving may no longer be advisable. Most state motor vehicle departments or local senior services organizations can provide assessment programs that help a person make a decision about whether to cut down on driving or give it up altogether. When that happens, there are certain steps that can help. A change in medications may help improve symptoms so that the person can continue to drive safely. If not, public transportation such as buses, taxis, or subways may be an option. Shuttle services for people with disabilities, offered by community groups, religious institutions, or senior centers, are available in many communities. Friends, family, or neighbors may be able to help with transportation. Carpooling with others may also be an option.

Nutrition Issues with PD

A healthy, balanced diet, with plenty of nutrients, fiber, and water, is important for anyone. There is no special diet for people with PD, but PD does present some health issues that make diet and nutrition even more important. For example, some studies have demonstrated an increased risk of osteoporosis, or bone thinning, in people with PD. As PD progresses and falls become more common, the risk of bone fractures goes up. PD patients need a diet that is rich in bone-strengthening nutrients such as calcium, magnesium, and vitamins D and K. Dehydration—from a lack of adequate fluid intake—is also common among PD patients. Dehydration is a serious health issue, responsible for almost 2 million hospital days per year in the United States. Dehydration in PD patients can worsen confusion, weakness, balance problems, bowel function, and kidney problems.

Some symptoms of PD can significantly interfere with eating and nutrition. For example, PD can slow the movement of the large intestine, which leads to constipation and abdominal discomfort. Hand tremors can make it very difficult for PD patients to manage eating utensils. Many people with tremors are embarrassed to eat with others because it is hard for them to cut their food or keep foods on their spoon or fork. They may get frustrated and give up trying. Cognitive and emotional symptoms of PD may cause a person to forget how to prepare meals or even forget to eat altogether. Depression may lead to loss of appetite and lack of energy to prepare food. These issues can often be improved or resolved by talking to the doctor and modifying or adding medications or other therapies so that the symptoms do not interfere as much with eating properly.

PD medications often have side effects such as nausea or loss of appetite that can interfere with proper nutrition, especially if several medications are being taken. Levodopa, for example, tends to work better when taken on an empty stomach,

A PD patient is assisted to drink. Difficulty drinking can cause dehydration, which can worsen confusion, weakness, balance problems, bowel function, and kidney problems.

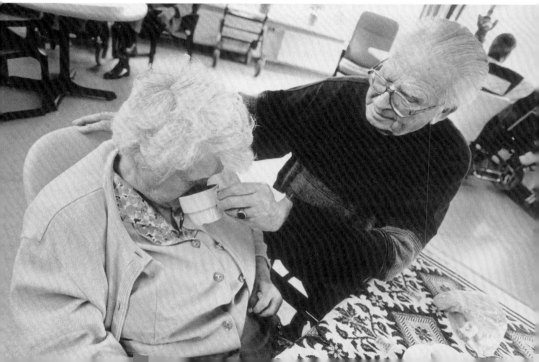

but this can cause nausea. In addition, levodopa and protein compete with each other for absorption in the intestine, so having them in the stomach at the same time can interfere with the absorption of both of them.

To alleviate these problems, medications can be timed so that they do not coincide with mealtimes. Many people also benefit from taking smaller, more frequent meals throughout the day. Nausea can be prevented by avoiding heavy, spicy, or greasy foods and by taking in food and drinks slowly. Resting after meals with the upper body elevated also helps prevent nausea. If nausea persists, the doctor can prescribe an anti-nausea medication.

Many PD patients have problems with chewing and swallowing due to loss of control of the muscles involved. Swallowing problems increase the chance of aspiration—accidentally inhaling food or liquids into the lungs. Aspiration can lead to a serious lung problem called aspiration pneumonia. Swallowing problems can be evaluated by a speech pathologist, who can make recommendations about ways to alleviate them. Meanwhile, there are ways to make swallowing easier and safer, such as sitting upright during and for fifteen minutes after meals, not talking while eating, taking smaller bites and chewing slowly, eating softer foods, and paying attention to swallowing.

Sleep and Rest

Like good nutrition, good-quality sleep is important for anyone's health and well-being. PD patients often feel fatigued and out of energy, so it is important to get enough good-quality sleep at night, along with periods of rest during the day. More than 75 percent of PD patients, however, report problems with sleep. Some are caused by the symptoms of the disease. Others are caused by side effects of PD medications. Sleep problems can affect the spouse or caregiver of the PD patient as well as the patient herself or himself.

Insomnia—trouble falling asleep or staying asleep—is one of the most common sleep problems in PD. Some people have trouble falling asleep when they go to bed. Others fall asleep but wake up during the night or very early in the morning and cannot get back to sleep. Insomnia can be caused by depression or anxiety, or it can be a medication side effect. Sometimes it is caused by symptoms such as tremors or muscle rigidity returning during the night after the last daily dose of medication has worn off.

Sleep apnea is a condition in which the muscles and tissues of the back of the mouth and throat relax at night and obstruct the flow of air through the air passages. It results in short periods during which the sleeping person stops breathing. It can cause loud snoring, restless sleep, and headaches and sleepiness during the day. About 40 percent of PD patients experience sleep apnea. Most people with sleep apnea are overweight, but this is not the case in PD. Even PD patients of normal weight are more prone to sleep apnea than those without PD. Sleep apnea is diagnosed with a sleep study that records a person's breathing patterns during sleep. It is treated with a CPAP machine.

Restless legs syndrome is a condition that causes unpleasant tingling, jerking, or cramping in the legs, along with the urge to move them. It happens most often at night and can wake the person up. People with PD are at a higher risk of experiencing restless legs syndrome, as well as another condition that often accompanies restless legs syndrome called periodic leg movement disorder.

REM sleep behavior disorder (RBD) is a sleep disorder in which people experience vivid, realistic dreams and may act out their dreams while sleeping. The REM (rapid eye movement) phase of sleep is the part of the sleep cycle during which dreams occur. Normally, only the eyes move during REM sleep. RBD can cause a person to talk, shout, grind their teeth, or kick or punch their bed partner during sleep. About 50 percent of PD patients experience RBD at some time, and it often occurs years before PD is even diagnosed. RBD can be treated with medication. Safety measures such as padded side rails on the bed or sleeping in a separate room may be necessary.

The DriveWise Program

DriveWise is a program developed at Beth Israel Deaconess Medical Center in Boston, Massachusetts, that provides an extensive evaluation of driving ability for people with physical, neurological, and psychiatric disorders. It is designed to help patients and families with the difficult decision of when to give up driving for safety reasons.

The program begins with a visit from a specially trained social worker, who talks with the person about how driving fits into his or her life and how giving it up might impact his or her life. An occupational therapist evaluates the person's visual, cognitive, and physical abilities, after which an on-the-road evaluation is done of the person's driving abilities. After the road test, the social worker and the occupational therapist meet with the person and his or her family to decide on the best course of action to take regarding driving. If everyone agrees that giving up driving is the wisest thing to do, the social worker helps with practical and emotional support and with finding workable alternatives.

All of these sleep problems can cause excessive sleepiness during the day, which is a problem in itself. Daytime sleepiness can also be a side effect of some PD medications. Although excessive daytime sleepiness becomes more common as people age, it is a significant problem for about 15 to 20 percent of PD patients, compared to only about 1 percent of the healthy elderly population. A person who is excessively sleepy during the day cannot participate in normal daily activities. They may have sudden sleep attacks in which they fall asleep suddenly, which can be very dangerous to the person as well as to others. In addition, sleeping during the day further interferes with the person's ability to sleep normally at night.

Sleep issues should be brought to the attention of the doctor so that they can be managed appropriately. "To that end," says

Aleksandar Videnovic of the National Parkinson Foundation's Center of Excellence, "patients and caregivers should write down a detailed overview of their symptoms and give these to their physician. Then, a medication review should follow to determine whether adjustments need to be made. Finally, a consultation with a sleep specialist and an overnight sleep study may be necessary."[24] Some other things that PD patients can do to help with sleep issues include maintaining a regular

Excessive daytime sleepiness (EDS) becomes more common as people age and is a significant problem for about 15 to 20 percent of PD patients.

schedule of going to bed and getting up, getting exercise and sunlight earlier in the day, decreasing fluid consumption late in the day to avoid having to get up to go to the bathroom at night, avoiding caffeine and heavy meals late in the day, and taking sedating medications later in the day to decrease day-time sleepiness.

Becoming a Caregiver

When Rick Weeden was diagnosed with young-onset PD more than thirty years ago, the doctor delivered the news rather bluntly, says Rick's wife, Betty. "It could be a lot worse," the doctor said. "Deal with it."[25]

PD profoundly affects the life of the person who has it, but it also has a significant impact on those who care for them. As the average age of the population continues to rise, more and more people will find themselves providing full- or part-time care to a spouse, parent, sibling, or friend with PD. Most care-givers are women, and most are over age fifty. Many are the adult children of the PD patient, with families and careers of their own to manage.

Caring for a person with PD can be expensive, time-consuming, and extremely stressful and frustrating, especially as the illness moves into its later stages. It often becomes a full-time job, one that may last for many years. Caregivers often find themselves taking on everyday tasks such as paying bills, cooking, cleaning, shopping, laundry, and driving the person to appointments. They must often help the person with bathing and grooming, eating, walking, and taking medications. They may have to cope with the person's emotional disturbances, memory loss, and mood swings. Lizabeth Muller says that since her father's diagnosis, "my mother has done an amazing job caring for my father. She was recently diagnosed with Alzheimer's, so being my father's caregiver takes an added toll on her. She shaves him. She cooks. She tries to walk him around. She holds him up. Mind you, this woman is 92 pounds and 4'8"!"[26]

For many caregivers, caring for a PD patient while also tak-ing care of the needs of their own family and work obligations can easily become overwhelming, especially if they have little or no help from others. Emotionally, it is very difficult to watch a loved one decline in this way and know that there is nothing that can be done to stop it. Caregivers may neglect their own physical and mental health for the sake of their loved one. They may find themselves becoming overstressed, quick to anger, irritable, and even depressed. They may become isolated from friends and social contacts. They may develop health problems of their own such as high blood pressure, fatigue, anxiety, insomnia, and loss of appetite. These are all signs of caregiver burnout. It is critical for caregivers to seek help and support from all available sources.

Help for Caregivers

The first step that caregivers and other family members can take once the diagnosis is made is to learn as much as possible about PD. Even though its progression is unpredictable, getting educated about the disease can help caregivers be prepared for and deal with whatever may come. Reading available material about PD, frequent contact with health professionals involved, and simple time and experience can help the caregiver adapt and cope with the demands of caring for a loved one with PD.

Community resources and support services are a valuable source of help and support for the family and friends of a PD patient. There are many different kinds of community support services available. They can provide education, financial assistance, emotional support, and in-home help so that the person can stay in his or her own home and the caregiver can get a much-needed break. Senior centers and adult day care providers can help care for the person during the day, providing meals, medications, and social activities so that caregivers can get to work and care for themselves and their family. Many community services provide transportation and physical or occupational therapy.

Support groups for PD patients and their families are present in most communities. These groups provide a valuable source of emotional support, information, and advice, shared

Dopamine and the Sleep Cycle

There are two basic states of sleep—REM and non-REM (NREM) sleep. NREM consists of four stages, numbered 1 to 4. Each stage lasts from five to fifteen minutes. A typical sleep pattern includes a period of NREM sleep followed by a very short period of REM sleep. Stage 1 NREM sleep is very light sleep. Many people feel a sensation of falling during this stage, which causes a sudden muscle contraction called hypnic myoclonia. In stage 2 the heart rate slows and body temperature decreases. Stages 3 and 4 are called slow-wave, or delta, sleep and are deep levels of sleep. In these stages the body repairs itself, strengthens the immune system, and stores memories. Each period of NREM sleep is followed by a period of REM sleep. Each REM period lasts longer than the one before. During REM sleep there is heightened brain activity, and the most intense dreams occur then.

The role of dopamine in the sleep cycle was not understood well until a study published in June 2006 showed that dopamine receptors on a part of the brain called the pineal gland increase in number early in the morning and decrease at night. The pineal gland produces a hormone called melatonin that triggers sleep. When dopamine receptors on the pineal gland increase just before morning, however, the production of melatonin is decreased, signaling the body to wake up. In PD, dopamine levels are low, so dopamine's effect on melatonin is not as strong, and people can experience difficulty waking up and staying awake during the day.

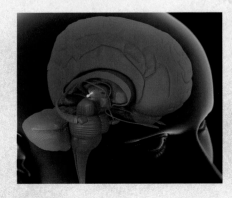

The highlighted area of the brain shows the pineal gland, which regulates sleep cycles.

among a group of people who are all having a similar experience and understand what caregiving can be like. They provide a safe place for people to share their deepest concerns and most troubling problems and to get suggestions from others who have dealt with the same challenges successfully. Most groups meet in person, once or twice a week. Others may meet by telephone, Skype, or online support groups such as the Parkinson's Information and Exchange Network Online. Some organizations—such as the National Alliance for Caregiving, the National Family Caregivers Association, and the Family Caregiver Alliance—provide workshops and meetings for caregivers to learn about PD and new ways to manage and cope with its demands.

Since Rick Weeden's diagnosis, neither he nor his wife, Betty, have let PD interfere with enjoying life to its fullest, traveling, camping, biking, and sailing. "Caregivers don't realize how strong they are,"[27] Betty explains. Even with her strength, however, she has realized that she cannot always do it all. Nursing assistants help her with Rick three days a week. This

Community resources and services, such as this support group, are a great help to the family and friends of PD patients.

has allowed her time to join a support group for caregivers, socialize with friends, and enjoy her hobby, quilting.

Lizbeth Muller is also getting the help she needs from a loving and supporting family. She says:

> Watching both my parents be so brave has been an inspiration. They will soon be moving in with me, so I can help care for them with the help of my siblings. My sister lives nearby and my brother, who lives in another state, provides his support as much as possible. I am fortunate to have my parents and I feel lucky that my family is very close. I think it's important for families to work together in the face of Parkinson's and create a solid support system.[28]

Difficult Decisions

As PD moves into its later stages, some difficult decisions may have to be made. One of the most difficult conversations that a caregiver might have with his or her loved one concerns the decision to stop driving. Often, the caregiver is the first one to notice issues that might make driving too dangerous for the patient. The caregiver may notice driving habits such as driving too fast or too slow, getting lost easily, ignoring traffic lights or signs, drifting into other lanes, or stopping for no reason. At this point, it may be time to talk with the person and his or her doctor about getting the patient's driving skills assessed and making a plan for alternative forms of transportation. Even if the person continues to drive, he or she may need restrictions such as driving only during the day or in good weather or taking only short trips. If the person is very resistant, the caregiver may need to resort to taking the keys away or removing the car from the home.

Eventually, the demands of caregiving may become too much to manage, even with help and support. It may be that financial resources run out, or the caregiver's health may be suffering too much to continue. Family relationships also may suffer due to the stress. At this point, it may become necessary to consider moving the loved one into a retirement community or skilled nursing facility, in which the person can get the care he or she needs twenty-four hours a day. This decision can be very difficult for caregivers because many people see it as "giving up" on their family member or abandoning them. The primary consideration, however, is the health, safety, and well-being of the patient and the caregiver. Factors to consider when choosing a facility include the cost, the location of the facility, its reputation for quality of care, the services available, and the competence and caring attitude of the doctors and staff.

CHAPTER SIX

The Future of Parkinson's Disease

Parkinson's disease is an area of intense interest among the medical research community, especially as the average age of the population increases and PD becomes more common. Although much has been learned about PD since the 1950s, there is still much to learn, especially in the area of causes, diagnosis, and treatment. To hopeful PD patients and their family waiting for discoveries and breakthroughs, the research process can seem painfully slow. Scientific research is necessarily time-consuming and costly, but there are no shortcuts. New treatment methods must go through a lengthy process of testing before they can be deemed safe and effective for use. The urgent need to find treatments and cures for illnesses must be balanced with the need to avoid undue risk or harm to the patient caused by using a new method too soon. Currently, a great deal of research at all levels is being done to learn more about PD—its causes and potential ways to prevent it, new ways to make more accurate diagnoses, and safer, more effective ways to treat the disease.

Finding the Cause—Genetics

A great deal of current research on PD is focused on gaining a better understanding of its causes, so that ways can be found to treat it and help prevent it. Currently, most theories about what causes PD center on genetic factors, environmental factors, or combinations of the two. One area of research that focuses on genetic factors examines the role of the PARK2 gene, which is often associated with young-onset PD. Research done in 2013 revealed the structure of the gene, which helps scientists understand just how mutations, or "mistakes" in the structure of the gene, lead to inherited forms of the disease. The PARK2 gene contains the code for making the parkin protein, which normally functions to protect neurons from damage. Mutations in the gene cause the parkin protein to malfunction so that it is unable to perform this task, and cell death results. The researchers discovered that when they made a mutation in one part of the PARK2 gene, it stopped working, and when they made a mutation in another part of the gene, it actually worked better. The research is important because the PARK2

A medical researcher uses human DNA from stem cells to conduct Parkinson's research. Research into the PARK2 gene indicates that it may serve as a biological indicator, or biomarker, for identifying people prone to developing PD.

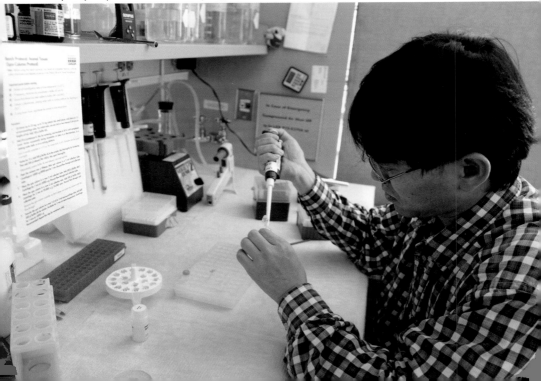

mutation may serve as a biological indicator, or biomarker, for identifying people prone to developing PD and because it suggests that drugs might be developed that make the PARK2 gene work better to protect neurons.

Related to this is the discovery that young-onset PD tends to progress more slowly than traditional PD, even though it begins earlier in life. The motor symptoms are not as severe, and they are controlled better by levodopa. Patients with inherited PD also keep their cognitive abilities longer and are less likely to develop PD-related dementia than patients with traditional PD. This knowledge can help patients who have the PARK2 mutation to be better informed about their disease and be better prepared for their future. For example, they will not have to worry as much about PD-related dementia and loss of cognitive functions.

Environmental Causes

Research is also being done on possible environmental causes of PD. For example, a 2013 study at the University of California showed that people who were exposed to one or more pesticides that interfere with a human enzyme called ALDH were three times more likely to develop PD than unexposed people. (ALDH detoxifies dopamine-related toxins.) If the exposed people also had a genetic variation in their ALDH, their risk was five times higher. Having the genetic ALDH variation alone, without pesticide exposure, did not increase the risk. The results of this study seem to confirm the theory that pesticide exposure combined with genetic factors can increase a person's risk for developing PD. It suggests that it may be possible to develop therapies that either boost the action of ALDH or detoxify the pesticides.

Although scientists and doctors understand what happens in the brain to cause PD symptoms, they still do not fully understand why or how the process actually begins. A new theory about what causes PD to start concerns the alpha-synuclein protein, the protein that in PD and other illnesses forms the abnormal clumps called Lewy bodies that damage the brain's neurons. Studies in mice have suggested that Lewy bodies have the ability to spread to cells in other parts of the brain and cause normal alpha-synuclein to become abnormal.

In the study the mice were injected with abnormal human alpha-synuclein. After four weeks there was no sign of the human alpha-synuclein, but there was abnormal mouse alpha-synuclein present. Four months after the injection, the mice began to show signs of cell death, which got worse over the next seventeen months. The test was repeated in macaque monkeys, whose brains are very similar to human brains, with the same results. The research confirms the theory that abnormal alpha-synuclein can spread to other cells and cause the normal protein to become abnormal. This may help explain why PD worsens over time. It also has implications for the development and testing of new neuroprotective therapies that can help protect neurons from the damage caused by Lewy bodies in the brain.

Neuroprotection

Several recent studies have suggested that certain substances may have some protective ability against PD. For example, one substance that may have neuroprotective qualities is caffeine, found in coffee, tea, and some sodas. The effects of caffeine in PD patients was first discovered during studies looking at risk factors for PD. Researchers discovered that people who had consumed caffeine over their lifetimes seemed to have a reduced risk of developing PD. Later studies focusing on caffeine seemed to support this conclusion. "Several large studies have carefully examined populations of patients, and all have uniformly concluded that higher caffeine intake seems to be closely associated with a reduced chance of developing Parkinson's disease,"[29] says Michael S. Okun, national medical director for the National Parkinson Foundation.

Another study from 2012 looked at the use of caffeine to counteract the sleepiness associated with PD. Although the caffeine did not improve the sleepiness, the researchers discovered that the study participants who received caffeine

The Research Process

Scientists, physicians, and government agencies work together to make sure that new drug treatments are safe and effective through a process of basic research, animal testing, and clinical trials in human subjects. Basic research is conducted in laboratories by scientists and is done to learn more about biological processes related to a particular disease. If basic research uncovers a promising new treatment, scientists then test it in laboratory animals to make sure it is safe for possible testing in humans. Animal testing can take several years. Drugs are tested for effectiveness, for any effects on other body organs, and to determine the best dosage.

If a drug proves to be safe and effective in animals, it moves on to clinical trials in humans. Human testing is done in several phases. In Phase I the drug is given only to healthy young volunteers and is tested only for safety. If the drug passes Phase I, it moves to Phase II, in which it is tried for safety as well as effectiveness in a small number of patients who have the disease for which the drug is intended. These patients are monitored very closely for all possible effects of the drug, good and bad. In Phase III the drug is tried in a much larger patient population, in a variety of different situations—in patients in the early stages of an illness, in those in a later stage, or in patients with different sets of symptoms—to see how the drug behaves in different patient scenarios. If any problems show up, more testing is needed before the drug can be approved for use.

Once the trials are done, the drug company submits all the data to a regulatory agency such as the Food and Drug Administration (FDA). If the drug is approved by the FDA, it is put on the market for doctors to prescribe for their patients. Even after a drug is marketed, monitoring for safety and effectiveness continues in Phase IV studies.

rather than a placebo (a "drug" that does not actually contain any medication) showed an improvement in their symptoms. This suggests that caffeine may also have a benefit as a treatment for PD as well as being a protective factor. "These results

Research indicates that regular intake of caffeine, found in coffee, cola, and tea, seems to be closely associated with a reduced chance of developing Parkinson's disease.

suggest an intriguing symptomatic benefit," says Okun. "The mild motor benefit of taking 100mg–200mg of caffeine twice daily seemed to be real. The true importance of this most recent caffeine study will be in helping to spur the development of new drugs and new targets for the treatment of Parkinson's disease."[30]

Other research is examining the possible protective quality of including berries as a regular part of a person's diet. A 2012 study, which followed more than 130,000 men and women over twenty years, found that people who ate two to three servings of berries per week were almost 25 percent less likely to develop PD than people who had less than one serving a month. Berries are a potent source of flavonoids—strong antioxidants found in fruits, vegetables, red wine, tea, and apples that help protect cells from the effects of oxidative stress. This may be the reason for their protective benefits. Interestingly, the benefits of consuming dietary flavonoids seemed to favor men rather than women. Men who had a high intake of many flavonoid-rich foods were 40 percent less likely to develop PD, but the same result was not seen in women.

Another substance that may have some protective benefit is nicotine, one of the chemicals found in cigarettes and other tobacco products. A 2011 study from the Federation of American Societies for Experimental Biology (FASEB) used genetically engineered mice to show that nicotine had the ability to preserve, or "rescue," dopaminergic neurons in the brains of the mice. Researchers caution against the use of smoking as a delivery system for nicotine, however, because of its well-known health risks. "If you're a smoker, don't get too excited," says Gerald Weissmann, editor in chief of the *FASEB Journal*. "Even if smoking protects you from Parkinson's, you might not live long enough to develop the disease because smoking greatly increases the risk for deadly cancers and cardiovascular diseases. But now, we should be able find non-toxic ways to hit the same target."[31]

Improving Diagnosis

Currently, there is no specific blood test or imaging study that can provide a sure diagnosis of PD. Diagnosis depends mostly on observation of the symptoms over time. Getting an accurate diagnosis this way can take a long time, and it also depends on the skill and experience of the doctor at recognizing PD symptoms. Research is being conducted to find new and better ways to get a quicker and more accurate diagnosis, so that patients and families can get their questions and concerns addressed sooner and so that treatment can start earlier in the course of the disease.

Researchers at the National Institute of Neurological Disorders and Stroke in Bethesda, Maryland, are looking for biomarkers—biological signs such as genetic mutations, biochemical imbalances, or other signs such as sleep or behavioral disorders—that may indicate an increased risk of developing Parkinson's disease. Early symptoms may also be biomarkers. For example, scientists have determined that PD tends to progress faster in people whose early signs include problems with balance and walking rather than tremors. Identifying at-risk individuals in this way has several major advantages. It provides a way to test new protective therapies by using them in susceptible people, to see whether the therapy protects them from developing the disease. If a person who develops symptoms of the disease is found to have one or more biomarkers, a quicker and more accurate diagnosis can be made.

A 2013 study, funded by the Michael J. Fox Foundation and conducted at several research centers, found that people in early stage PD may have lower levels of four different proteins in their spinal fluid. Measuring the levels of these proteins may serve to confirm (or rule out) a diagnosis and may help predict the course of the disease in people with this kind of biomarker.

Another study conducted at Emory University in Atlanta, Georgia, and at the University of California–Los Angeles (UCLA) found that people with fast-progressing PD had significantly higher levels of a chemical called N8-acetyl spermidine in their blood than patients with slower-progressing PD. "The course of Parkinson's can be highly variable," said Beate Ritz, a professor at UCLA's Fielding School of Public Health and one of the senior authors of the paper. "Some patients can become wheelchair-bound, demented or severely depressed within just a few years after diagnosis, while others are spared for longer periods."[32] If N8-acetyl spermidine turns out to be a biomarker for fast-progressing PD, it may help doctors diagnose the disease earlier and more accurately, predict its pattern of progression, and treat it more effectively.

Another interesting study, reported in early 2014, expanded on a previous discovery that Lewy bodies are not only present in the brains of PD patients, but are also found in nerve cells in the salivary glands located under the lower jaw, called submandibular glands. In this study twelve biopsies (tissue samples) were taken from the submandibular glands of people who had had PD for five or more years. Nine of them showed Lewy bodies in these glands. This was a very small study, and further research using healthy subjects as well as PD patients needs to be done, but it showed that submandibular gland biopsy may be useful in diagnosing PD in its earlier stages.

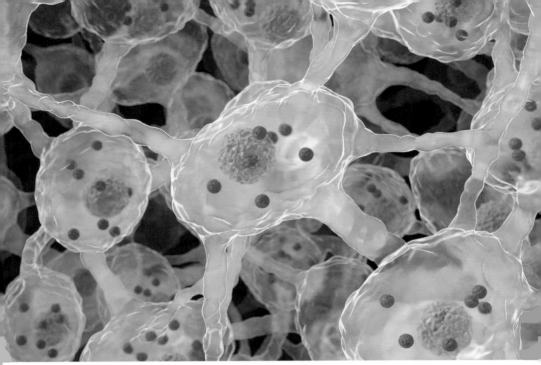

Lewy bodies (orange spots), typically found in the brains of PD patients have recently been found also in their salivary glands, which means that a relatively easy biopsy of these glands could help diagnose PD.

Research into PD biomarkers is a very exciting area of study because of the potential of biomarkers to revolutionize PD diagnosis and treatment. "Our hope," says Ritz, "is that such biomarkers may aid in earlier detection and more effective disease management, and that they will lead to new prevention strategies and improved clinical trials for new treatments based on a better understanding of how the disease progresses."[33]

Advances in Drug Therapies

The majority of research in Parkinson's disease treatment centers on drug therapy. According to Pharmaceutical Research and Manufacturers of America, there are currently thirty-seven different drugs either in clinical trials or awaiting review by the U.S. Food and Drug Administration (FDA). Twenty-three of them are for the treatment of PD itself, eleven are being developed for treatment of Parkinson-like conditions, and three are designed for diagnostic testing purposes.

Acupuncture, Bees, and PD

Acupuncture is a form of traditional Asian medicine that has been used for many centuries. Traditionally used to treat pain, it involves the insertion of very fine needles into specific areas of the skin. According to ancient tradition, acupuncture works by rebalancing the body's life force, or chi (pronounced "chee"), which flows through the body along pathways called meridians. Acupuncture has been used for many years in Asia to help with PD symptoms. Recent research at Kyung Hee University Hospital in Seoul, South Korea, tested whether acupuncture, and specifically acupuncture done with bee venom, is actually effective for controlling PD symptoms.

Patients in the study were divided into three groups. One received traditional acupuncture. Another received acupuncture along with injections of bee venom under the skin at the needle sites. The third group (the control group) received no treatment. Symptoms improved in the first two groups but not in the control group. Researchers theorize that bee venom may paralyze small muscles, similar to the way botulinum toxin (Botox) does, and therefore help relieve muscle spasms and tremors. It may also be that acupuncture helps increase dopamine levels in the brain. More research is needed, though, to confirm the results.

Researchers say bee venom may help relieve muscle spasms and tremors in PD patients by paralyzing small muscles.

PD drugs are designed to increase the levels of dopamine in the brain in order to control the symptoms. Currently, the most effective drug therapy uses carbidopa-levodopa combination drugs. Although they are highly effective, they are not perfect. "This drug has significant limitations," says Tanya Simuni, a professor of neurology at Northwestern University in Chicago. "It is very short-acting. In the early stages of Parkinson's disease, the brain can compensate, but as the disease progresses, this becomes increasingly difficult, and symptoms start to re-emerge."[34] The drug can also wear off during the night, and symptoms can return and interfere with sleep.

A new way to deliver the drug may be able to help with the problem of the drug's wearing off during the night. Studies are currently being done to evaluate the effectiveness of a gel form of carbidopa-levodopa that can be administered directly into the intestinal tract by means of a surgically implanted pump. With this delivery method, the patient does not have to worry about taking oral medications several times a day, and the pump provides a steady dose of the drug so that symptoms are controlled better.

Sometimes drug treatments for one disease are found to have benefits for patients with other diseases as well. This is what happened when Jean-Martin Charcot discovered that hyoscyamine, which he had been using to treat drooling, also helped relieve the motor symptoms in people with shaking palsy. In 2013 scientists discovered that a drug called nilotinib, which has been used since 2007 to treat adults with leukemia (a form of cancer of the white blood cells), reduces levels of abnormal alpha-synuclein protein and improves motor symptoms in the brains of mice that have been genetically engineered to have PD. Since nilotinib has already been tested and approved for treating leukemia, this could speed up its approval for use in PD if further research confirms these early findings.

Other research is looking at ways to decrease the unpleasant side effects of PD drugs, especially the most commonly used one—levodopa. For example, one of the most distressing side effects for patients is dyskinesia, the uncontrollable movements of muscles, which is different from the resting tremors of PD. Dyskinesia can make it very difficult to do even the simplest things, such as sitting still or walking, and can cause a person's body to move in distorted ways or cause the arms or legs to jerk uncontrollably. A study conducted by centers in several countries found that an overactive nerve pathway inside neurons, called the Ras-ERK pathway, was the cause of dyskinesia. By blocking two of the proteins involved in the pathway, its activity could be "turned down" to reduce the dyskinesia. "We have shown that altering the levels of a protein called Ras-GRF1, which specifically activates the Ras-ERK pathway in nerve cells, directly affects the severity of dyskinesia in a mouse model," says Riccardo Brambilla of Cardiff University in the United Kingdom. "This tells us that drugs which target the Ras-ERK pathway have huge potential as future treatments."[35]

Research is also being done to find new and better drugs to treat specific symptoms of PD, particularly in its advanced stages. For example, as many as half of all PD patients eventually suffer from significant psychotic disorders such as hallucinations and delusions. Traditional treatment for this involves antipsychotic drugs, which can worsen the motor symptoms of PD and cause other very serious side effects. A new drug called pimavanserin appears to be effective for PD psychosis, without the side effects of traditional drugs. Patients in the study who received the new drug also slept better, were more wakeful during the day, and had improved mental functioning, which was also very helpful for their caregivers. Pimavanserin is also being investigated for use in psychosis associated with Alzheimer's disease and schizophrenia.

Gene Therapy

Many human illnesses are caused by the malfunction of one or more mutated genes that are responsible for a particular function in the body. Gene therapy is a way to treat or even prevent a disease by replacing defective genes with normal genes in the affected body part or by inactivating mutant genes so that they cannot perform abnormal functions. It can also be used to introduce new genes that can fight the defective ones.

A new kind of gene therapy, called ProSavin, helps control motor symptoms in PD patients. ProSavin works by reprogramming brain cells to produce dopamine. It also helps even out the ups and downs of symptom relief caused by the short-lived action of levodopa. ProSavin uses harmless, inactivated viruses to carry three different kinds of genes that program for dopamine production into the brain. The genes can convert neurons that do not make dopamine into neurons that do. "We demonstrated that we are able to safely administer genes into the brain of patients and make dopamine, the missing agent in Parkinson's patients," said researcher Kyriacos Mitrophanous, head of research at Oxford BioMedica in England. Hoping to improve on their results, the researchers have since re-engineered the therapy. "We have a new version which makes more dopamine in patients, and this new version is undergoing safety studies before we initiate trials in patients."[36] Gene therapy is not a cure for PD, because brain cells continue to die, but it is hoped that gene therapy can help stall the progression of the disease for several years.

Nerve Cell Transplantation

Nerve cell transplantation has become an area of great interest in the surgical treatment of PD. The idea of transplanting cells into the brain began in the 1980s. At that time the interest was in transplanting cells from the adrenal glands, rather than nerve cells, into the brain of PD patients. The adrenal glands are located at the back of the abdomen, just above each of the kidneys. Although they are quite small, they have several important functions. They produce several hormones, such as adrenaline, that affect human growth and development, determine responses to stress, and help with kidney function, blood pressure, blood sugar metabolism, and secondary sexual characteristics. The hope was that the adrenal gland cells, once implanted into the brain, would continue to produce chemicals that the brain could convert to dopamine. The procedure had

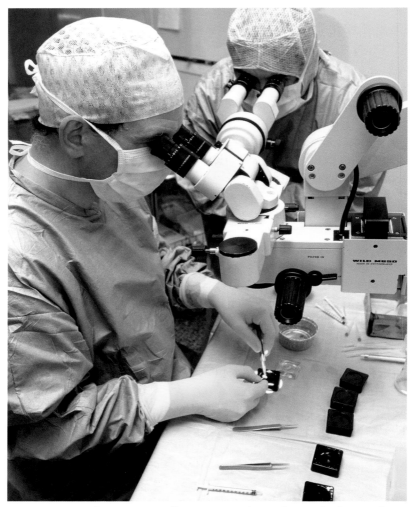

Doctors transplant nerve cells. Once implanted into the brain, they will continue to produce chemicals that the brain will convert to dopamine. Such transplants may prove therapeutic for PD patients.

its difficulties, however. It required two separate operations, one in the abdomen and one in the brain. It was lengthy, risky, and ultimately was not shown to produce long-term benefits. It is no longer done today.

The concept of transplanting nerve cells into the brain is similar. Most of the interest in this has involved transplanting human fetal nerve cells into the brain of the PD patient in the hope that the fetal cells would be able to take over the function of lost dopaminergic neurons in the brain. This procedure is still experimental and so far has not been proved to provide significant long-term benefits to PD patients. In some patients, in fact, it seems to cause worse movement problems, a complication known as runaway dyskinesia. The lack of a clear benefit to the patient, the risks of runaway dyskinesia, and the ethical issues surrounding the use of fetal cells mean that much more research is needed before fetal cell transplantation can be widely used. Meanwhile, substitutes for human fetal cells, such as cells from other animals, is a subject of ongoing research.

Nerve Growth Factors

Another area of research interest involves nerve growth factors, also called neurotrophic factors. Nerve growth factors are chemicals in the brain that help neurons grow and survive. One of the more important nerve growth factors for dopaminergic neurons is called glial-derived neurotrophic factor, or GDNF. It is hoped that the use of GDNF might help prevent dopaminergic neurons from dying off, help reduce symptoms, and maybe even slow the progression of PD. Currently, however, the use of GDNF also has its problems. It is a very large molecule and cannot cross the blood-brain barrier, so it cannot be taken by mouth or injected into the blood. Instead, it must be implanted directly into the brain. So far, methods of doing this have not worked well in people (although it seems to work well in laboratory monkeys).

Work with GDNF continues, however, with researchers experimenting with different dosages and different delivery methods. One promising new delivery method involves delivering "corrective" genes into the neurons themselves. Instead of implanting GDNF into the brain, the corrective genes are carried directly into the neurons by deactivated viruses that can get into the cells but cannot cause illness. Once inside the brain cells, the gene directs the cells to start producing GDNF or other chemicals that can improve dopamine function and relieve PD symptoms. So far, this kind of gene therapy has been shown to have some beneficial results without causing harm to the patient.

Stem Cell Therapy

Stem cells are primitive cells that have not yet developed into any particular kind of specialized cell. They are like a "blank" cell, with the potential to become any kind of cell, such as a muscle cell, stomach cell, or neuron. Stem cells can be converted in the laboratory to almost any kind of specialized cell. They can then be used to treat diseases or injuries by replacing damaged cells. Stem cells that are converted into dopaminergic neurons, for example, could theoretically replace damaged neurons in the brain and actually repair the damage caused by PD.

Stem cells can also be used to create disease models, which can be used to learn more about disease processes and test new treatment methods. For example, in a 2013 study at the University of California–San Diego, scientists took stem cells from a person with an inherited form of PD (involving a mutation in the gene that codes for the alpha-synuclein protein) and created neurons, some with the gene mutation and some without it, and then exposed them to various pesticides. The healthy neurons were not affected by the pesticides. In the abnormal neurons, however, the cells' mitochondria—the "energy factories" of a cell—malfunctioned and produced high levels of cellular "pollution." The research demonstrated how environmental toxins can trigger neuron damage in people with a genetic predisposition to such disorders.

Stem cells can come from several places. Some stem cells are obtained from human embryos in the earliest stages of development. These stem cells are called pluripotent stem cells, which means that they can become any kind of cell in the body. Other kinds of stem cells can be found in blood drawn from a newborn's umbilical cord after birth or from several kinds of tissues in the adult body, such as bone marrow, muscles, the heart, and even the brain. These adult stem cells are called

A Spicy Treatment

One of the major aims of PD research is to learn more about what actually happens in the brains of PD patients, so that new treatment methods can be developed that target those specific discoveries. Using this kind of knowledge, scientists at Rush University Medical Center in Chicago, Illinois, have discovered that cinnamon, commonly used as a food flavoring and preservative in many parts of the world, can reverse many of the changes that occur in the brains of mice with Parkinson's disease.

After it is taken in, cinnamon is metabolized in the liver to form a chemical called sodium benzoate. Sodium benzoate is already used as a drug to treat certain kinds of liver diseases. The researchers found that sodium benzoate, which can cross the blood-brain barrier and enter the brain, can stop the loss of important brain proteins such as parkin, protect neurons from damage, stabilize levels of neurotransmitters, and improve motor symptoms in mice. If these results can be replicated in people with PD, it would represent a major advance in safe and effective treatment for PD.

multipotent, which means that they can become any kind of specialized cell, but only from the part of the body from which they came. For example, stem cells from bone marrow, where blood cells are made, can become any kind of blood cell.

Another source of stem cells are human-made stem cells called induced pluripotent stem cells, or iPS cells. First discovered in 2007, iPS cells, like embryonic stem cells, are able to become any kind of cell type. iPS cells are created in the laboratory by converting a mature cell into a state that is more like an embryonic stem cell. Scientists continue to work on ways to produce adequate amounts of strong stem cells, from all sources, that can survive and function fully inside the brain for the treatment of PD.

Parkinson's disease diagnosis, treatment, and management have come a very long way since James Parkinson's time. "I think James Parkinson would marvel at the progress that has been made in diagnosing, understanding, and treating the condition that now bears his name," says PD researcher Patrick Lewis. "But I'm sure he'd be surprised and disappointed to discover that, almost two centuries after his essay, we are yet to find a cure for this devastating condition."[37] Still, scientists, doctors, and, most of all, patients, refuse to give up working to find a cure. "I am very optimistic," says Paola, the young woman who was diagnosed with PD at age fifteen, "and I believe that the medicine has so many advances that the cure is going to be found! Don't let the off periods stop your life, fight against them and prove to them that you are strong! Just live the most of every day and smile!"[38]

Notes

Introduction: The Shaking Palsy

1. Homer. *Iliad*, Book XXIII, trans. Richmond Lattimore. Great Books. Vol. 3. Chicago: Encyclopedia Britannica, 1951, p. 285.
2. Quoted in Rob Stein. "Leonardo's Letter Debunks Theory Parkinson's Is Caused by Pollution." *Los Angeles Times*, March 6, 1989. http://articles.latimes.com/1989-03-06/local/me-188_1_leonardo-letter.
3. Quoted in Donald Calne. "What Triggers the 'Shaking Palsy'?" *Cerebrum* (blog). Dana Foundation, April 1, 2002. http://dana.org/Cerebrum/Default.aspx?id=39219.

Chapter One: What Is Parkinson's Disease?

4. Rich Clifford. "An Astronaut's Journey with Parkinson Disease." National Parkinson Foundation. www.parkinson.org/Personal-Stories/An-Astronaut-s-Journey-with-Parkinson-Disease.
5. Clifford. "An Astronaut's Journey with Parkinson Disease."
6. Emily Deans. "Dopamine Primer." *Psychology Today*, May 13, 2011. www.psychologytoday.com/blog/evolutionary-psychiatry/201105/dopamine-primer.
7. William J. Weiner, Lisa M. Shulman, and Anthony E. Lang. *Parkinson's Disease: A Complete Guide for Patients and Families*. 3rd ed. Baltimore, MD: Johns Hopkins University Press, 2013, p. 10.
8. Paola. "Making Dreams into Reality." American Parkinson Disease Association National Young Onset Center, 2011. www.youngparkinsons.org/stories/paola.
9. Paola. "Making Dreams into Reality."
10. Paola. "Making Dreams into Reality."

Chapter Two: Causes and Symptoms

11. Weiner et al. *Parkinson's Disease*, p. 20.

12. James Parkinson. "An Essay on the Shaking Palsy." All AboutParkinsons.com. www.allaboutparkinsons.com /essay-on-the-shaking-palsy.html.
13. Frankie Miller. "Spirit of Giving." National Parkinson Foundation. www.parkinson.org/Personal-Stories/Spirit -of-Giving.
14. Parkinson. "An Essay on the Shaking Palsy."
15. Margaret M. Hoehn. "The Five Stages of Parkinson's Disease." Parkinson's Resource Organization, January 17, 2012. http://parkinsonsresource.org/wp-content/up loads/2012/01/The-FIVE-Stages-of-Parkinsons-Disease.pdf.

Chapter Three: Diagnosis of Parkinson's Disease

16. Quoted in Ashley Jost. "Parkinson's Fight Inspires Couple to Help Other Sufferers." *Springfield (MO) News-Leader*, June 29, 2014, p. 11A.
17. Quoted in Jost. "Parkinson's Fight Inspires Couple to Help Other Sufferers."
18. Weiner et al. *Parkinson's Disease*, p. 115.

Chapter Four: Treating Parkinson's Disease

19. Calne. "What Triggers the 'Shaking Palsy'?"
20. Quoted in Brenda Goodman. "Deep Brain Stimulation May Offer Lasting Benefits for Parkinson's Disease." WebMD, August 8, 2011. www.webmd.com/parkinsons-disease/news /20110808/deep-brain-stimulation-may-offer-lasting-benefits -parkinsons-disease.
21. Quoted in Sara Calabro. "Complementary and Alternative Parkinson's Treatments." Everyday Health, June 2009. www.everydayhealth.com/parkinsons-disease/alternative -parkinsons-disease-treatments.aspx.

Chapter Five: Living with Parkinson's Disease

22. Lizbeth Muller. "I Want My Father to Dance at His 65th Wedding Anniversary." National Parkinson Foundation. www.parkinson.org/Personal-Stories/I-want-my-father-to -dance-at-his-65th-wedding-anni.

23. Quoted in Dan Crace. "Walking." National Parkinson Foundation. www.parkinson.org/Personal-Stories/Walking.

24. Aleksandar Videnovic. "Sleep and Parkinson's Disease." *Parkinson Report*, Summer 2011. www.parkinson.org /NationalParkinsonFoundation/files/ac/ace94f62-e0fe -40a5-bfc4-3200b2628543.pdf.

25. Quoted in Betty Weeden. "A Caregiver Heroine in Fiction and Real Life: Betty Weeden." National Parkinson Foundation. www.parkinson.org/Personal-Stories/A-Caregiver -Heroine-in-Fiction-and-Real-Life--Bett.

26. Muller. "I Want My Father to Dance at His 65th Wedding Anniversary."

27. Weeden. "A Caregiver Heroine in Fiction and Real Life."

28. Muller. "I Want My Father to Dance at His 65th Wedding Anniversary."

Chapter Six: The Future of Parkinson's Disease

29. Michael S. Okun. "Caffeine as a Potential Treatment for Parkinson's Disease." National Parkinson Foundation, August 2, 2012. www.parkinson.org/Patients/Patients ---On-The-Blog/August-2012/Caffeine-as-a-Potential -Treatment-for-Parkinsons-.aspx.

30. Okun. "Caffeine as a Potential Treatment for Parkinson's Disease."

31. Quoted in Federation of American Societies for Experimental Biology. "Nicotine Can Protect the Brain from Parkinson's Disease, Research Suggests." *ScienceDaily*, August 1, 2011. www.sciencedaily.com/releases/2011/08/110801111738 .htm.

32. Quoted in University of California–Los Angeles. "Researchers Find Chemical Signature for 'Fast' Form of Parkinson's." *ScienceDaily*, November 22, 2013. www.sciencedaily.com /releases/2013/11/131122103938.htm.

33. Quoted in University of California–Los Angles. "Researchers Find Chemical Signature for 'Fast' Form of Parkinson's."

34. Quoted in Norra MacReady. "Improving Parkinson's Disease Treatment Through Research." Everyday Health,

June 10, 2009. www.everydayhealth.com/parkinsons
-disease/treatment-research.aspx.

35. Quoted in Parkinson's UK. "Putting a Stop to Dyskinesia,"
    May 2013. www.parkinsons.org.uk/content/putting-stop
    -dyskinesia.

36. Quoted in Steven Reinberg. "Gene Therapy May Hold
    Promise for Advanced Parkinson's Disease." WebMD,
    January 9, 2014. www.webmd.com/parkinsons-disease
    /news/20140109/gene-therapy-may-hold-promise-for
    -advanced-parkinsons-disease.

37. Quoted in Parkinson's UK. "Dr. James Parkinson." www
    .parkinsons.org.uk/content/dr-james-parkinson.

38. Paola. "Making Dreams into Reality."

Glossary

akinesia: The absence of movement, or the inability to move.

alpha-synuclein: The protein that, in its abnormal form, collects into clumps called Lewy bodies in brain cells and causes neurological diseases such as PD and Alzheimer's disease.

axon: The long, tail-like projection from the body of a neuron that sends electrical messages to other cells.

basal ganglia: A collection of small structures in the base of the brain that have many important functions, including regulating muscle movement.

bradykinesia: Abnormally slow movement.

cognitive: Related to mental processes such as thinking, learning, memory, attention, reasoning, logic, decision making, and problem solving.

dendrite: Small projections on a neuron that receive incoming electrical messages from other neurons.

dopamine: A chemical neurotransmitter in the brain that is largely responsible for regulating muscle movement and is decreased in PD.

dopaminergic: Related to neurons that produce dopamine.

dyskinesia: Abnormal and uncontrollable muscle movements, different from tremors. A common side effect of long-term use of levodopa.

dystonia: Uncontrolled and sometimes painful muscle spasms that turn or twist body parts; especially common in the feet.

idiopathic: Of unknown cause.

Lewy bodies: Abnormal clumps of protein found in the brain neurons of people with PD, Alzheimer's disease, and other neurological diseases.

mutation: A "mistake" or abnormality in a gene that causes the gene to express its function abnormally and can cause many human disorders.

neurological: Related to the nervous system.

neuron: A nervous system cell that transmits electrical messages from the brain to other body cells.

neurotransmitters: Chemicals or hormones that carry messages from cell to cell and affect a large part of human function and behavior.

oxidative stress: The process of cell damage associated with cell death and the aging process.

parkinsonism: The set of symptoms that includes tremor, bradykinesia, postural instability, and muscle rigidity, seen in several kinds of neurological diseases.

postural instability: Difficulty maintaining balance and upright posture.

substantia nigra: A small structure in the brain, part of the basal ganglia, that is damaged in PD.

synapse: The gap between neurons and other cells across which messages are transmitted by neurotransmitters.

tremor: The uncontrolled shaking of a body part such as a hand, arm, or leg, seen in several neurological disorders such as PD.

Organizations to Contact

American Parkinson Disease Association (APDA)

135 Parkinson Ave.
Staten Island, NY 10305-1425
(718) 981-8001; toll-free: (800) 223-2732
Young Onset Center: (877) 223-3801
www.apdaparkinson.org

The APDA provides patient and caregiver support with more than one thousand support groups, education and positive lifestyle programs, social and fund-raising events, and scientific research funding at all levels. The association also features the National Young Onset Center for younger PD patients.

Michael J. Fox Foundation for Parkinson's Research

Grand Central Station
PO Box 4777
New York, NY 10163
(212) 509-0995
www.michaeljfox.org

The Michael J. Fox Foundation was founded by and named for Canadian actor Michael J. Fox, who was diagnosed with young onset PD in 1991. The foundation provides millions of dollars for PD research, with the goal of eliminating Parkinson's disease.

National Institute of Neurological Disorders and Stroke (NINDS)

PO Box 5801
Bethesda, MD 20824
(800) 352-9424
www.ninds.nih.gov

The mission of the NINDS is to seek knowledge about the brain and nervous system and to reduce the burden of neurological disease. The NINDS supports and conducts research, trains and educates researchers, and communicates new discoveries to the public, scientists, health-care professionals, and government agencies.

National Parkinson Foundation (NPF)

200 SE First St., Ste. 800
Miami, FL 33131
(800) 473-4636
www.parkinson.org

The NPF supports research, care, and support services for PD patients and their families. The foundation's goal is to improve care through research, education, and outreach.

For More Information

Books

Alan M. Hultquist and Lydia T. Corrow. *Can I Tell You About Parkinson's Disease? A Guide for Family, Friends, and Carers.* London: Kingsley, 2013. A book about PD as told by Nikolai, a fictional character with PD. Good for younger readers.

H.P. Newquist. *The Great Brain Book: An Inside Look at the Inside of Your Head.* New York: Scholastic, 2005. Provides in-depth information about the inner workings of the human brain, presented in an entertaining and easy-to-read style.

Shelley Schwartz. *Parkinson's Disease (300 Tips for Making Life Easier).* New York: Demos Health, 2006. Provides tips for helping those with PD and their caregivers adapt to PD and live full, happy lives. Written by someone who has multiple sclerosis and understands the challenges of living with a neuromuscular disease.

Michael Tagliati. *Parkinson's Disease for Dummies.* Hoboken, NJ: Wiley, 2007. Part of the Dummies series of informational books, this comprehensive and clearly written book offers information about PD, along with techniques for coping with daily issues and providing care as the disease progresses.

Websites

American Parkinson Disease Association National Young Onset Center (www.youngparkinsons.org). Provides a wealth of information about young-onset PD, as well as help on how to manage life with YOPD through newsletters, blogs, and personal stories.

National Family Caregiver Association, Caregiver Action Network (www.caregiveraction.org). Provides valuable information and resources for caregivers of people with a wide range of conditions who require full-time care.

National Parkinson Foundation (www.parkinson.org/Parkinson-s-Disease/PD-Library/Web-Sites). Includes information about all aspects of PD, including legal and financial information for patients and families, a PD library, and informational videos and webcasts.

Parkinson's Disease Health Center, WebMD (www.webmd.com/parkinsons-disease/default.htm). A comprehensive site with information about PD, its causes, symptoms, diagnosis, treatment, and daily management. Includes news about research as well as a community page for those living with PD.

Index

Picture Credits

About the Author

Lizabeth Craig worked for thirty-five years as a registered nurse before leaving the profession in 2013. She holds a bachelor of science in nursing from the University of Florida and a bachelor of science in secondary education from Southwest Missouri State University. She began writing as a "serious" (but really a lot of fun!) hobby in 2002 and has since published numerous stories and articles for children and adults. In 2007 she began writing books for Lucent Books; *Parkinson's Disease* is her thirteenth. She lives in Springfield, Missouri, with her husband, Richard, tabby cat Rosie, and dogs Molly and Maggie.